A BEAUTIFUL LIFE

Spiritual Wisdom
for
Everyday Living

A BEAUTIFUL LIFE

Spiritual Wisdom
for
Everyday Living

Question & Answer Series

Book 1

Sri Avinash Do

Published by Sri Avinash Do Mission Inc

A Beautiful Life: Spiritual Wisdom for Everyday Living
Question & Answer Series Book 1
Copyright © 2017 by Sri Avinash Do Mission Inc

ISBN: 978-0-6480076-2-3

Published by Sri Avinash Do Mission Inc, Australia
www.SriAvinash.org
admin@SriAvinash.org

Printed and bound in India

*This book is dedicated
to all those whose hearts
are searching for comfort,
upliftment and awakening
to their Divine Self.*

Contents

Introduction

A Beautiful Life: Spiritual Wisdom for Everyday Living is a collection of Spiritual Master Sri Avinash Do's responses to seekers' questions at his public talks between August 2015 and February 2016, conducted at his Self-Realization Ashram in northern NSW, Australia.

Some of the questioners display an innocent curiosity about spirituality, while others are struggling with how to bring peace and fulfillment into their life. Yet others express a deep yearning for spiritual understanding and practical guidance on their journey.

In his characteristic fashion, Sri Avinash uses everyday language, stories from his own life, and original parables to share practical wisdom with his audience. He responds to each question with clarity and passion, gently redirecting each soul away from the troubles of their mind and the world, back home to their true spirit—where peace and happiness can become their everyday experience.

By contemplating what Sri Avinash shares here, readers will be able to absorb the deeper meaning and spirit behind his simple words. Through this greater understanding, they will be inspired to live the life that they have always longed for—a happy and purposeful life.

—Sri Avinash Do Mission Inc, June 2017

Part I
Essential Truths

"Suffering is only in the realm of the body and the mind. The soul, the spirit, doesn't have any suffering. It is always free."

Who am I?

Is it important on the spiritual path to ask the question 'Who am I?'

It is important. You should ask the question 'Who am I?' particularly in moments of great forgetfulness of the love and the beauty in yourself. Moments when you are in anguish, moments when you are drowning emotionally. Moments when you can't find one person on the planet who actually loves you or understands you—that type of spiritual loneliness, not just physical loneliness. Moments that you are feeling totally depressed, like there's nothing to live for. Moments when you feel you just can't do it, you just can't go on like this. Moments of your deepest fear.

It is in these moments that you should ask yourself, 'Who am I?'

Who am I? Am I weakness? Am I fearful? Am I scared and shallow and nasty and lacking? Am I that? Who am I?

Or am I a child of God, created in the image and likeness of God? Am I this indestructible being? Am I this fearless being— fearless of life and fearless of death? Am I infinite love and strength and courage? Who am I?

You should ask these questions especially in those drowning moments, because it is then that you need to know the answer the most.

Then, having that mindset, you should ask these questions in every moment. Not just when you're in darkness and forgetfulness, but when you are in great joy and bounce and dance and light and calm and love. You should ask yourself in every moment, 'Who am I?'

The answer? I must be beauty. I must be magnificence embodied. I love life. I love God. I love my existence. I love who I am and where I am, and who I am with or who I am not with. I love it all.

Love

How can we start to feel love when we feel no love in our life or in ourself?

If your drink bottle is empty, what do you do? You fill it up.

If you feel like you have no love, then that means you feel empty of love. So what you need to do is fill up that bottle. Fill yourself with love.

And thank God for this one ultimate truth—that we're all one. Because if we don't know how to fill this love in us, all we have to do is be loving and kind towards others. And not just a person—it could be an animal, nature, a butterfly, anything.

When you do that, because we're all one with everything, suddenly the love that you give to another fills up your own bottle.

What is love?

I can tell you what love is not. Love is not a discussion, love is not a study, love is not a game.

Love is just love. We all know what love is. Have the courage to live it.

Can we not see love in our life? Have we not experienced love? Of course we have. When we were born we were the embodiment of love. The way your mother or father first looked at you—they were in love with you.

You've experienced love. In your heart you know what love is. Nothing can take that away.

So that is not the issue—not knowing what love is.

The issue is we need to live this love, express this love, every moment in our life. That's the issue. Not that we don't know it. Instead of expressing love we express fear. We express too much fear.

But I didn't come to this planet to define love. I came to this planet to encourage the love that we know in our hearts—to express that more, to live that more.

Happiness

What is happiness?

True happiness is when you know you need and want nothing— and you still have an innocent grin on your face. That's happiness!

Feeling flat and unmotivated

What can we do when we just feel flat and unmotivated on the spiritual path?

When you feel flat and unmotivated that is a good sign, because then you know change is needed. Otherwise how do you know change is needed?

It's only when a car has a flat tyre that you know you have to change that tyre. If you don't know the tyre's flat and you keep driving at 100 km/hr around a bend, it is dangerous.

So flatness can be a good thing, it can save your life, it can lead to happiness.

Unhappiness in the world

You've mentioned several times in your satsangs that people are in misery, but are people really that unhappy?

We are living at a time on our planet where there is misery and unhappiness occurring on a mass level. The only reason why it doesn't look like that is because nobody wants to admit it.

But if we were truthful, if everybody on this planet had the courage to be transparent, every problem would be solved.

If we were transparent, when a person is feeling suicidal, they'd print out two signs with bold lettering saying, 'I feel suicidal'. They'd stick one on their chest and one on their back. Then a person who feels lonely will put an 'I feel lonely' sign on their chest and their back too.

If everyone did this, then we'd all look at each other thinking, "Huh—you're suicidal? I didn't know that!" And someone looks at you thinking, "Huh—you've got bipolar? I didn't know that!" The supermarket manager's sign says, 'I'm massively depressed'. And in the fruit section, the person putting out the apples has a sign saying, 'I have regular anxiety attacks'. When the CEO of the company comes to visit the store their sign says, 'I hate myself, I have no love for myself'. Then everyone will feel, "Huh? This is the CEO and they're not well either!"

If we all saw each other like that, we would realise, "There's something going on. Why is everybody like this?" Then we'd do something about it.

But our planet is not transparent like that. If we have some sort of illness or if we're suicidal or if we're taking tablets for depression, we don't want other people to know, in case they judge us.

But if the whole world was transparent like that, once in a while someone's sign might say, 'I haven't felt sad or low for years. I feel beautiful every moment of my life!' It might be a bus driver, and when he finishes his shift and goes to the supermarket, everybody will be saying, "Huh? There are 100 people here and everybody has got some problems except this one guy."

Now, those 100 people won't want to let the bus driver leave until they've asked him, "How do you do that? How come you're like that?" And then he will share, "Well, it's because of this... It's because of that... I live like this... My perspective is like that..." So then those 100 people will adopt that same approach and, after some years, everybody comes to the supermarket and they all have new signs saying, 'I love myself and other people'! The situation will change.

But we're not living in a society where we're allowed to be transparent. Imagine going for a job interview and you have a sign saying 'I hate myself'. The company manager will say, "Look, I've got plenty of people wearing those signs, I don't need another one." You won't get the job! We're living in a society like this.

I feel the sooner we are honest about the scale of mental illness and suffering that is currently occurring on our planet, the quicker we will work together to put an end to our suffering and misery.

The cause of suffering

Why is life so miserable for some people?

Because they were told and conditioned how they should be and how they should live, instead of being taught to be themself. So they feel, "I am living a false life."

I'll share a robust example.

It's like a person who is size extra extra large and they wear underpants in size extra extra small. They will have some sort of suffocation!

But in this case it's spiritual suffocation. They're living falsely. Their soul is so expansive but they just fit themself into this conditioned mind, because they're believing what they were told about who they are.

So they're believing that, they're living that, and they're expressing that.

Now, let's say a man who is size extra extra large is walking around wearing extra extra small underpants for 70 or 80 years—I can tell you, that person will feel uncomfortable!

So what we have to do is fit right. When someone is extra extra large, they should wear extra extra large underpants!

Because our soul is as expansive as the universe, we should fit that expansiveness. We shouldn't be limited. Our suffering is caused by that chokingness of the limitations and conditions we hang on to.

So we have to live our true Self, live that expansiveness. Our mind should be as expansive as the whole universe. Then we'll feel, "Ah, this way of living is really comfortable. This fits me really well."

So that is the reason why we're suffering. We've been told who we are, how we should live, how to be—and it's just the wrong size.

Get your size right, and then you'll be happy.

Attachment to outcomes

Often we wish to have a certain outcome, so we work towards that, but if it doesn't turn out we feel disappointed. How can we work wholeheartedly towards something without being attached to the outcome, so that if it doesn't happen it's OK?

I could say many things about this, but really it comes down to our life experience. We all have enough evidence in our lives to know that when we do something with expectation, it's potentially a set-up for disappointment.

For example when you really want a job, you do everything right at the interview and have a good connection with the interviewer, but for some reason you don't get the job— disappointment. But when you have no expectation, if you don't get the job, you're not disappointed.

So from our life experience, we know we should do everything without thinking about whether we're going to get it or not. We should go through the whole of life like that. But it's not easy, because when we go through life and have no expectation, the problem is then we won't do anything at all! We've only got two modes—we expect to achieve something, then we just go for it, or we don't expect anything, so we don't bother taking any action.

So we can see that it's not easy to take action without having expectations. Theoretically it sounds great, but to be able to live it is another matter.

The best way to do that is dive through life fearlessly—try your best with all your effort, and know that the outcome is in God's hands, not yours. And know that God loves you and God will give you the best outcome.

When you have that type of knowing and trust as you go through life, you will know that whatever happens, "This must be the best for me." That's the perfect attitude for peace of mind.

I'd like to share a beautiful story I've heard about this.

There was a king who was very close to his assistant. The assistant was sincere, loyal, and peaceful.

And one day, somehow, the assistant accidentally cut the king's finger. The king said, "You've cut my finger! I might get an infection. This is terrible! What do you think about this?" And then the assistant said, "Well, I think God does everything for the best."

The king said, "What do you mean God does everything for the best? Are you saying that it's good that I got cut? I got hurt and you're saying that's for the best?"

So the king started to have doubts about his assistant—maybe he had other motives, maybe he didn't really care for the king. And because the king didn't trust the assistant anymore, he kicked him out of the palace. The assistant struggled to get a job and became a beggar, living in the street.

Some time later, the king went for a walk in the forest and was captured by a wild clan. The king was so healthy and so well-fed that they wanted to use the king as an offering for their ritual.

They tied the king up, all ready to burn him, and suddenly in that moment the chief said, "No! We can't go ahead with this ceremony! The king is not perfect—he's got a scar on his finger. We cannot do the ritual with an imperfect offering."

So they untied the king and let him go.

Then the king sent his army out to find his old assistant. When they found him, the king said to him, "You nearly died in the street, starving to death, after you were so loyal and faithful to me. That cut on my finger saved my life. What are your thoughts about me sending you away like that?"

And the king's assistant said, "Well, I think God does everything for the best, because if you didn't send me away I would have been with you and then they would have sacrificed me instead!"

So you can see that that assistant's attitude was perfect. He was not upset with the king when the king sent him away onto the street like that. He just trusted that everything is perfect—God does everything for the best. So he was very peaceful.

So that's how we become peaceful. We should march forward through life having no expectations.

Letting go or holding on?

Does success on the spiritual path come from letting go or from holding on?

It's both. You want to let go of your egotism, and you want to hang on to love.

You want to hang on to the love of God, you want to hang on to the love of humanity, you want to hang on to the love of nature, you want to hang on to the love of the rainbow, you want to hang on to the love of your family, you want to hang on to the love of your Master, you want to hang on to the love of your friends. Hang on to the beautiful things!

And let go of everything else—let go of your mind.

So you hold on and you let go too.

Wisdom

What is true wisdom?

True wisdom is knowing what actions lead to beauty and what actions lead to being trapped in the hole of suffering.

Knowing the difference, and living that way—that's wisdom.

How does one come to gain wisdom?

By learning from someone who already has that wisdom.

In the same way, how does a champion tennis player become a champion tennis player? They didn't just rock up to Wimbledon and say, "I want to win Wimbledon today." They learned from another champion tennis player.

So in the same way, you learn wisdom from someone who has wisdom, such as a great Spiritual Master.

Meditation

What is the essence of meditation?

Stillness of mind—when the energy within you is calm and still.

A rock may show outer stillness, but meditation is when the energy *within* you is still. You have no thoughts. That stillness is called the 'state' of meditation.

Meditation techniques are tools, but the meditation state is really just stillness of mind. No thoughts.

If you look at the mind, it's like a pendulum on a grandfather clock—left, right, left, right—it's moving. Stillness is when the pendulum stops moving altogether. When the mind is completely still, then that's called meditation.

If the meditation state is not about being physically still, could you talk about how we can achieve things and do things while being in that state?

You see, it's about inner stillness. It's not outer stillness.

A good example of that is—imagine a glass of water. If you can move it very gently, without shaking it, the glass of water is moving but you will notice that the actual water is very still.

In the same way, we can have outer movement in our body—like walking or running—but we can have inner stillness.

Or, we can have outer stillness but there's inner movement—you can be still on the outside, but inside your thoughts are moving. Thoughts are just pure energy, so when you're thinking, it creates energy movement. For example, you could be sitting down practising a meditation technique and your body is very still—you're not going anywhere, you're not moving—but inside your mind is racing. You're thinking of what you can put on Facebook! You can't wait to make a comment on your friend's post. That's inner movement.

The goal is to have inner stillness. And from that inner stillness then outer movement or outer non-movement is irrelevant. When you don't move outside, when you sit still, there's beauty and magnificence and peace in that. And when you walk, there can be grace in that, when you talk, there can be grace in that—as long as there's stillness inside.

If you meditate by concentrating on one point—like your breath or the sound of a bell—how does that actually stop thoughts?

Because concentration is awareness, thoughts cannot enter when your awareness is focussed on one point.

For thoughts to enter, your awareness has to be dissipated, not concentrated. It's like a torch light that spreads out and doesn't focus on one point, so its light is weaker. It is that weakened awareness that allows the possibility of thoughts to enter.

If anybody wants to switch off their thoughts, then concentration will do that.

For example, if you concentrate on the breath, you can't think at the same time. As soon as you lose concentration, you will think. And then when you concentrate again, thoughts will stop. So meditation is using techniques to concentrate on one point.

What you're trying to do during the period of meditation is concentrate for as long as possible, so that thoughts don't come. When there are no thoughts, you are able to experience the beauty of oneness, or non-separation consciousness. So if you can concentrate for long durations, then you literally start to experience oneness for longer periods. That's a very good thing for your life. And if you do it for longer, longer, longer—minutes and hours and days—then before you know it you're the master of concentration. You're the master of meditation.

When you master it like that you can flick away any thoughts easily. You can turn off thoughts like you're turning off a light switch. Then, if someone's rude to you and your mind starts to think, "He is so rude!" you just switch that thought off and you won't be disturbed by it.

But if you can't concentrate, then you've got no chance—thoughts will control you. Your life will look like the tail wagging the dog. Your life won't be at peace.

So a meditation technique is a way to develop this concentration. If you concentrate on your inner chakras, that's called chakra meditation. If you concentrate on what's happening around you in each moment, they call that mindfulness meditation. If you concentrate on the sound of a mantra, they call that mantra meditation. If you concentrate on spaghetti, they call that spaghetti meditation. But don't tell people you do spaghetti meditation!

Renouncing the world

Is it necessary to renounce the world to live a spiritual life? What does it mean to renounce the world?

To renounce the world means you let go of what's *not* who you are. You're letting go of things that don't represent you.

For example, if you haven't had a shower for a month, when you have a shower you wash off all the dirt that is not part of who you are. When you renounce, you renounce all the dirt in your mind that's not who you are—you let go of every false idea about yourself.

Sometimes you see a big tree and there are other plants nearby which climb all over it, blocking out the light and suffocating it. So to renounce is like cutting away all those climbing plants so that the tree can get the light again, can be itself.

This is the essence of a spiritual life, where every moment of every day you're striving to cut away all those vines that have latched onto that tree of yourself. In other words, all these ideas and concepts you have, which are known as 'conditioning'. Ideas like—I'm spiritual, I'm not spiritual, I'm rich, I'm poor, I like this, I don't like that, I'm creative, I'm not creative, I'm good at music, I'm not good at music.

When all these ideas are gone, you're left with nothing but purity, nothing but 24 carat gold with no other metals mixed in there. You're left with a quiet freedom.

Karma

What is karma?

Karma is the law of cause and effect. It is the backbone, or the skeleton, of the universe. That's just how the whole universe is structured—it's based on cause and effect.

What that means is when you cause suffering for another, the suffering will come back to you. And when you do something beautiful for another being, then the same beauty that you gave to them comes back to you. It's like a wheel—what you do spins around and comes back to where it started.

How can we free ourselves from karma?

To free ourselves from karma is to be beyond the body and the mind—beyond the material plane. When we realise our true Self, then in that moment we are beyond the law of cause and effect.

In practical life, a self-realised person won't have any emotional disturbance. For example, when a Master experiences a situation that most people would consider painful—which would cause them suffering—the Master won't see that as unfavourable. And because they don't see that as unfavourable, they don't have a reaction, and because they don't have a reaction, they aren't disturbed. And because they aren't disturbed, they don't feel suffering.

Suffering is only in the realm of the body and the mind. The soul, the spirit, doesn't have any suffering. It is always free.

Having negative thoughts

If I have a bad thought about somebody, can that hurt them?

If you have a bad thought about someone it will hurt them, but they may not be able to perceive it.

But just because they can't perceive it, it doesn't mean there's no impact, no damage. It's like parking your car at the shopping centre and somebody bumps their trolley into it. It's a tiny bump and you may not notice it for a while, but the damage is there.

All negative thoughts are fear-sponsored, not love-sponsored. So when you have a negative thought about someone, because it's fear-sponsored, you're giving a piece of your fear to them.

Very few people can guard against that—you've basically got to be a Master to be able to block off other people's fears from you. A Master is full of love, so when that fear comes towards them, their love will just swallow the fear and the fear will be transformed into love.

But when you still have fear in you, you won't be able to block that fear out. So when someone has negative thoughts about you, the negative energy will enter you, but you don't know. And then that leads to other effects, like you might be grumpy or you feel unsettled or disturbed. Or you might snap at someone, or feel anxious for no obvious reason at all.

When you know how that works, you will want to train your mind to be loving—to not have fear and negativity towards others. Negativity towards others will always lead to negativity about yourself. And the negativity about yourself will always lead to negativity towards others. So it becomes this vicious cycle of negativity—a tornado of negativity.

So be kind to others, love people, be compassionate. That way you're not causing hurt to another person—or to yourself.

What can I do to rectify the harm my negative thoughts have done?

What's done is done—what's said is said, what's thought is thought. The destruction has already happened, and once the cyclone has demolished the house, the house is gone. But even though the house is gone, you can always build a new house—a better house—by replacing it with beautiful thoughts, kind words, loving actions. This is the best way to rectify the harm that your negative thoughts have caused.

For example, when I was a spiritual seeker, sometimes I realised I missed an opportunity to be kind to someone— sometimes you just miss it. And why did I miss it? In that moment

I must have had a fear-sponsored, selfish thought that I wasn't aware of, otherwise I wouldn't have missed the opportunity to be kind.

So what would I do? I'd look for another person to be kind to. If I was in India, I may give some gifts to poor children or give up my seat on a crowded train—I'd do something good. So that fear-sponsored reaction was replaced by a love-sponsored action.

You don't have to do something good to the same person. Maybe the person has caught the bus so they're gone. But what's important to know is that if you're kind to someone else, in essence, that is the same as the first person benefiting, because we are all connected—we are all one.

You may be surprised, but sometimes just staying quiet and not reacting is actually the best way to be kind and loving towards a person. When someone's rude to you and you're calm and not reactive to that person, that's love-sponsored, because fear would have reacted negatively. And when you don't react, that is tremendously powerful—the impact is beyond imagination. Neither of you may realise it, but both of you will be changed forever.

So that's what you do. You just replace the negative thought with a beautiful thought, a kind deed, or loving words. Now, 'loving words' doesn't mean you run around telling everyone, "I love you, I love you." If you say that to the wrong person they might slap your face!

But the best way to rectify the harm that you have caused another by your negative thoughts is to be kind and loving—to the same person, or if you can't do that, to another person.

Forgiveness

How can we forgive if we can't forget?

The idea to 'forgive and forget' is really just a theoretical concept. In reality, if you can't control your mind, you can't forgive, even if you want to.

And when you're able to control your mind, even if you don't want to forgive, you can't do that either—you'll just forgive anyway!

So it's about whether you are able to control your mind or not. If you're able to control your mind then you won't be hurt. And if you're not hurt, then there's no need to forgive. Forgive what? If you're not hurt, you would not seek damages. You would not want the person to say sorry. You'll feel, "I love that person." You wouldn't think, "I forgive that person."

So forgiveness has to do with the ability to control your mind.

When somebody does something that you don't like, if you're able to control your mind, you can just let it go and not give it another thought.

If you want a definition of forgiveness, that is it.

Just saying the words, "I forgive you," doesn't really mean much. If you truly forgive, you won't even say that. You'll just respond with love. You'll just respond with peace. That is forgiveness—your peacefulness towards that person is forgiveness.

And 'forget' goes with it too, because the issue will not arise within you any more. You will naturally feel it's over—it's done and dusted.

Heaven

Is there such a thing as heaven?

Yes, there is. When I was young I would watch *Video Hits* on television, and I think Belinda Carlisle sang the song, *Heaven is a Place on Earth*. It's true—heaven is right here, right now. You're not going to find heaven anywhere else.

Heaven is living on earth and knowing that there's nowhere else you'd rather be, and there's nothing else you want to do but whatever you're doing right this moment. The right here, right now. The present moment—when you're totally grateful and content, without any expectation for something else to enhance your life. Now *that* is called heaven.

And when we haven't realised and lived and expressed that knowing, that's called hell. Then we'll be having expectations and discontentment and impatience and feeling like a failure.

So Belinda Carlisle is right! Heaven *is* a place on earth.

But hell is also a place on earth. It's all here, basically. Heaven and hell are both here on earth.

Death

What happens when we die?

The ultimate truth is there's no such thing as death. Anybody who has realised their true Self will know there's no such thing as death.

And if there's no such thing as death, then there's no such thing as birth.

Death and birth are just like you trading in your old car and bringing home a brand new one. Or throwing out your old set of clothes and putting on a new set.

So based on the understanding that there's no birth and death, we can see that after we die life just continues. We just get a new body. The shape of the body looks a bit different, like a new car or a new set of clothes, but we are the same soul inside that body.

For example, when you put on a different set of clothes today, did you feel that you were a different person from who you were yesterday? Did you feel you were reborn today? You didn't feel that, did you?

In the same way, from the soul's perspective, it doesn't feel like we are reborn. It feels like it's just another day we wake up to, or just another life.

Sin and virtue

What is the greatest sin and what is the greatest virtue?

The greatest sin is not knowing your magnificence, not knowing why you came to this planet, not knowing your aspiration, your love and excitement for this journey—and living a whole lifetime just surviving and suffering. That's the greatest sin.

And the greatest virtue is that somehow, living in a world of suffering, you actually remember your real nature and why you came to such a beautiful planet. In the midst of darkness and forgetfulness, you remember.

This remembrance is the greatest achievement—it's the greatest virtue in a human being. When your life is not a life of suffering anymore, your life becomes beautiful. And it's not just that *your* life becomes beautiful—everyone around you becomes beautiful as well. That's the greatest gift, the greatest virtue, and the greatest achievement that a person can have.

Selfishness

How can I be true to myself without being selfish?

When you are true to yourself, you could be a very selfish person—and when you are true to yourself you could be a very non-selfish person. Both could be true.

The question is, which 'self' are we talking about?

Is it the self that you think you are—what country you're born in, what family you're born in, your status, your job, your education, your experience, your beliefs, your intelligence, your mind, your body, your history, your past—is that the self that we are talking about?

Because if that's the self we're talking about, and if you're true to that self, you'll be a selfish person.

But if that's not the self we're talking about, if we're talking about the Self that is eternal, that is pure presence, that is awareness and emptiness and non-physicalness—then if you are true to that Self, there'll be no selfishness.

Because selfishness means that you only love and care for yourself and not for others. But your true Self, the eternal Self, sees there is no 'other'. Everything is itself. So it loves what we call 'another' like itself, because it loves itself. It will care for another, naturally—and that is what we call selflessness.

And when one is true to that Self, then selfishness or guilt about selfishness just won't happen.

Reading spiritual books

I find reading good spiritual books so calming and so beautiful sometimes. But is simply reading a book something that can actually transform our spiritual growth?

Yes and no. Some books can cause us disturbance and other books can be calming. So the issue is not 'books' or 'not books'—the issue is *what* books. And when we read those books, *how* we read them.

Let's assume we're reading beautiful, quality books that touch our heart, that bring us closer to our divine Self, and create remembrance in us. Now, how do we read those books? We can read those books as just further ideas, further information, further theory, further concepts—spiritual concepts in this case. But the goal is not to gather more concepts. The goal is to purify or let go of all the concepts that we've gathered throughout our life.

So it depends on the type of books we're reading and how we're reading them. Some books we read can give us more concepts, and other books that we read in the right way can destroy our concepts.

Good books will touch us deeply, and will help us remember the truth. There's a feeling of deepness and significance. And anything deep will destroy anything surface. So when you read a good book in that way, it will destroy all your surface weeds. Anything deep is like an oak tree—the roots go deep. No weeds can affect an oak tree.

So when you read a quality book, you should read it because it's beautiful—it just touches your heart, comforts you, makes you cry with longing, makes you love life, makes you hang in there, makes you open up, makes you love your Creator, makes you live your secret, makes you try your best, makes you strive to be good, makes you strong, makes you happy.

Read those books!

God

Who or what is God?

God is this being of love.

When you are loving, and you feel this sweet love in your heart towards all of life, then you'll know God.

You'll not know God by definition—you won't know God by reading about God on Wikipedia, you won't know God by being told about God.

You will know God through love. Once you love the whole of creation, then you'll know God. And you'll know God to be this being that is everything and everywhere.

In terms of the feeling, you just feel a closeness to this being that can't be put into words—this Divine Spirit, this sacred connection. You feel like you're in the arms of God.

If God is everywhere and everything, why is there so much pain and suffering in the world?

Because even though God is everywhere and everything, we have successfully done the impossible, to think that we are separate from God and live in this imagined box called our mind. Eternally we can't do that, so in that sense it's impossible. But in the short-term, we appear to have successfully achieved this division.

When I grew up in Tempe in Sydney, there was this little island—probably just 100m²—in the middle of Cooks River. So if we imagine God as Australia, it's like living on that island and thinking, "I'm not in Australia—I live on my own island. I've got my own country here."

Our mind has successfully divided everything, making us think we are separate from the whole of existence, from God. We're living in a cosmos that is in reality inseparable, where everything is interconnected—but we somehow manage to experience ourselves as separate beings. This is only true because of the instrument of the mind, and is just our perception. The mind is like computer software that generates experiences, but they're only perceptual experiences—they're not true reality. That is why ancient seers and living Masters—who can see reality—call our perception and experience of the world an illusion.

And in that illusory way of seeing things, God and the rest of the world are separate from us, in the same way that the person on the island thinks, "I've got my own island here. I'm not part of Australia." Thinking this way is what causes suffering—when we feel isolated and disconnected from other people and the world.

So we're the ones that have built the software, with our thoughts. We are the ones who put up these imaginary walls—made up of concepts and conditioning—that separate us from existence.

Therefore we're the ones that have to take these imaginary walls down, so we can reconnect with life and God. And because God is everyone and everywhere, to feel connected to life and God means to have love and compassion for all living beings. Then suffering in this world will truly come to an end.

How can I experience God in my daily life?

To answer this, I'd like to share a metaphor.

Most people eat three main meals a day—breakfast, lunch and dinner. When we haven't had dinner, when it's been delayed, somehow we very quickly remember—"Oh, I haven't had dinner yet. I better find something to eat." We seem to remember dinner very well. And lunch, and breakfast. First thing when we wake up, most people think, "What will I have for breakfast? Will I have toast? Will I have muesli and yoghurt? What will I have?"

So in the same way, we should think of God at least three times a day. It doesn't need to be four times—just start off with three and let it go from there, naturally.

Every time we feel the heavy burden of life, for example if we don't like our job or we have financial difficulty, we should think of God.

And every time we have a beautiful experience, like somebody tells a joke and cheers us up and makes us laugh, we should think of God.

We should think of God for everything—what we have, how lucky we are, what we don't have—it must all be perfect.

So in the same way that we can't live without breakfast, lunch and dinner, we should try to remember that we can't live without being close to God. Have the same attitude. Then suddenly you'll feel close to God. You'll think of God all the time. Everywhere you go, you'll feel God is your friend, God is your protector.

My life feels so hard at the moment. Is there any point in asking God or a higher power for help?

We all need help. I need help. Everybody needs help.

I'm sitting here answering a few questions, but I need help. I need somebody there to operate the video camera.

We all need help. So we should have the attitude that there's nothing wrong with that. It makes you feel humble. We shouldn't be ashamed.

So when we're in trouble, we should call for help. But when you have no-one around you to help you, who do you call out to?

Just imagine you're in the middle of the ocean and the motor of your boat breaks down. Now you need help. Your mobile phone is flat and you're just floating there. In that moment, who are you going to call out to for help?

I know in my life when I was in desperation I called out to God to guide me, to help me. I didn't even know how to pray!

And when I called out for help, help came.

So I suggest that when you need help, don't be shy—don't be afraid to call out for help to the best helper. Why do I say the 'best helper'? Because if you're drifting in the middle of the ocean, no-one can help you except God.

When people survive an earthquake and are rescued from the rubble, all you read about in the magazine is the story, 'Miraculous—someone survived for six days underneath the rubble.'

You don't hear how they were praying to God for help when they were underneath there. They were praying day and night. They were praying to God for help, for someone to find them.

In all circumstances, God is our best helper. And 'when you've got the best, then you can peacefully rest'.

So never be afraid to pray to God for help.

What pleases God the most?

When we're happy, it makes God happy. When we're sad, God feels sad. They say in some religions, 'God the Father', and they use the analogy of a father because it is very similar in some ways to our parents.

If a child goes to primary school and runs home feeling really happy, then the mother and father will feel happy. When the child comes home from school and they're crying because they've been bullied, their parents won't be happy. In the same way, when we are unhappy and we're suffering—crying in our bedroom—God feels unhappy.

So the first thing that pleases God the most is when we're happy.

The second thing that pleases God is when we cause happiness to other people. When we are understanding, kind, peaceful, loving and gentle towards other people, it makes God very happy.

And the third thing that pleases God is when we live our life in a way that is conducive to happiness—when we do things that make *us* happy.

So what are the things that make us happy? One example is hanging around with other people who are happy. When we do that, God will be happy. It's the same with our parents—when we hang around with people who are happy, our parents will be very happy. But if we hang around with people who get us into drugs and crime, and we end up in court—our parents won't be very happy!

So when we do things that actually make us happy, God becomes very happy. For instance spiritual practices such as prayers and meditation, cultivating kindness and compassion, having a helpful attitude—all these things will please God.

Even asking these questions will make God very happy, because it brings out the answers, the wisdom, that leads to our own and other people's happiness.

Following your heart

How can we discover our deepest intention in life?

By not settling for anything less than what our heart yearns for— no discounting, no compromising—and ruthlessly, beautifully, living that way.

We know when we compromise our heart. Let me share an example. Let's say in high school, Bill really wants Jenny to be his girlfriend. He loves Jenny and every time he talks to her it makes him feel beautiful. But he's afraid to speak to Jenny. Now, Susan happens to like Bill and so Susan asks her friend to ask Bill if he wants to be Susan's boyfriend. And Bill says, "OK."

That might sound like a slightly silly example, but it shows the compromise. It shows that what the person loved the most, yearned for the most, they discounted, and never pursued, and they settled for what they didn't wish for.

So don't settle for anything less than what your heart truly yearns for.

Do we all know what our heart loves the most?

If we don't look, we don't find. If we look, we will find.

We watched *The Truman Show* last night, and Truman looked and searched. He knew something was not quite right with his life, so he searched until he found it. He found a way out of the movie set he was in, out of that illusion.

When we search without giving up, we *will* find what our heart truly loves.

Is meditation a way to tune into your heart?

Meditation is one way to tune into your heart. But you can say it the other way around—if you tune into your heart you'll be in meditation!

In essence they are the same thing. You see, meditation is the state of no mind. It is the state of that eternal presence, the eternal now. And that is where the heart lies.

So if you want to be in your heart and know your heart, meditation is one way. Another way is to cultivate that warm, heartfelt, loving feeling.

But essentially, meditation and tuning into your heart are the same thing.

Seeing our body as a temple

It is said that our body is a temple, but at the same time we're guided to identify less with our body and more with our heart or soul. Should we look after our body like it's a temple?

When we identify with our true Self more and more, we will feel oneness and love with all of creation more and more. And because our body is a creation of God, we will feel grateful to 'lease' this body for however long we live. We naturally feel gratitude.

So we will take care of the body. We will treat this leased equipment with care. When the body is in a bit of pain we use herbal medicine, or acupuncture, or a pain killer—whatever medicine we use—to take care of it.

We don't thrash it, we don't poison it, because we feel grateful that it was lent to us from God. And because we love God, we love ourself, so we will take care of the body.

Now if we have a car, we know we should take care of it, but we don't spend two hours every day to polish it up to make it shiny, do we? We would make sure the tyres are not bald so we don't slide on the road and smash the car. We make sure the car is serviced. We check that the oil is not low so the engine won't get damaged—it costs a lot of money to replace the engine. We take care of it.

So to see our body as a temple is like that—we take care of it, but we're not obsessive about it.

Health

What's the cause of ill health and how can we best restore our health?

Step 1—stop eating junk food. Step 2—stop focusing on junk thoughts. Step 3—start an organic garden! And when you have that garden and you have plenty of veggies, give the abundance you have to others.

And the 4th step—learn how to be detached from your body. That means you don't worry about your body. You don't care if people call you 'fat', 'skinny', 'short', 'tall', whatever—you just don't worry.

Our body is naturally an absolutely magnificent thing. For example it knows how to naturally detox, and if you get a cut it knows how to coagulate the blood to quickly stop the bleeding. It's a self-healing system.

Even though our body is so robust, we should still be kind to our body. Try not to eat junk food and processed food, which create toxins that the body struggles to get rid of so they manifest in the form of diseases.

Disease is also produced by worry, anxiety and stress. These emotions release toxins that eat away at the body.

It's ironic to say, but if you want to live long and be healthy, you have to not worry about dying. In other words you have to be fearless. And when you're fearless, you're peaceful, because you're not nervous. And when you're peaceful, automatically you become wise, and when you're wise you're grateful—you won't throw junk in your body because you're grateful to your Creator.

Looking for happiness

It is said that in the world today we're looking for happiness in all the wrong places. Would you agree with that?

I guess all we have to do is look at the evidence.

If there are seven billion people on the planet, there are at least seven billion different strategies to become happy, because everybody is trying to be happy.

Some people try to become wealthy, others seek happiness through wandering all over the world backpacking, and some seek happiness through meditating in a cave. Some people go to the country for a more simple life. Some go in the midst of chaos and busyness to give them the best chance to seek happiness through fame—the next Tom Cruise or Arnold Schwarzenegger.

So you can see that if there are seven billion people, there are seven billion strategies to become happy.

But it all comes down to results. So if there are seven billion strategies and if we look at the total result of humanity, do we give it a Pass, Credit, Distinction or High Distinction?

A High Distinction is enlightenment.

A Distinction is the dog wagging the tail most of the time— pretty happy. Occasionally the tail wags the dog.

A Credit is you're happy most of the time, except when some unfortunate thing happens in your life which takes a little bit of time to get over—but you get over it.

A Pass is you're hoping that nothing bad happens in your life. You hope your girlfriend doesn't leave you, because you love her heaps. You hope you don't lose your job. You hope—fingers crossed! That's a Pass.

And a Fail is you feel life doesn't have a sense of beautiful purpose. Inside your heart you feel a sense of loneliness, you feel a lack of support, you feel that no-one loves you. You feel like you can't wait to be in an ideal situation in your life. You can't wait to win the lottery! And of course, there is depression and anxiety and all those conditions that plague this planet. Well that's an F. That's a Fail.

On the planet now we have the most sophisticated technology man has ever seen. We can send an email across the globe in a few seconds. We are using the latest technology in everything, and the most up-to-date, state-of-the-art knowledge. Even though that's the case, you tell me—what's the score? What did humanity get—the seven billion people? What do you think?

A big F. Everybody is trying to be happy, but the result in the world currently is a state of emotional disaster. This can be seen by the fact that in almost every single family on this planet there is at least one person who has some sort of mental illness such as anxiety, depression, etc.

So something is wrong.

However, there are people who are happy. There are people who get High Distinctions, there are lots of people with Distinctions, and lots more with Credits.

We should ask—how did they get Credits, Distinctions and High Distinctions?

We should search for these people then spend time with them—learn from them and copy them—and strive to get Distinctions and High Distinctions ourselves. Then one day we can graduate with a 'Bachelor of Being a Happy Human Being' too.

Developing gratefulness

Why do we take so many blessings for granted and how can we quickly drop that habit so we can treasure our blessings?

It's true that we take many blessings for granted. For example, our life itself is an amazing blessing, but we mostly don't recognise that.

You might be surprised by this, but one major reason we take our blessings for granted is because we're just too spoilt.

When all a person has is a few coins in their pocket, and they get a free meal, nobody needs to teach them how to be grateful. On an empty stomach, with no money to buy food, and suddenly somehow food appears so they can fill their tummy— automatically they will be full of gratitude in that moment! But if your belly is always full and then somebody gives you a free meal, it may not mean much to you.

So we don't take things with this feeling of gratefulness—we don't see life as such a blessing—because we're just spoilt. We take it for granted because we have too much.

A spoilt person is someone who has so much but feels they have so little, whereas a grateful person is someone who has so little but feels they have so much.

That's why one method of spiritual practice is to live with as little as possible. Like St Francis of Assisi said, be a friend of poverty—it can teach you so much.

In my life I experienced growing up with financial poverty, which made me so grateful. I'm so grateful that as a refugee from Vietnam I had an opportunity to come to such an abundant and beautiful country as Australia. I remember when I was 9 years old in the refugee camp in Malaysia and they announced that our family had been accepted by Australia, the feeling of gratitude was so overwhelming that we all got tears in our eyes.

I was blessed to come here, and now I feel, "I to want give something back in return, and dedicate my life for the benefit of others." And this is because I didn't have much. My mother died when I was three years old. My father was a fisherman who went out to sea working, so I hardly saw him. And then we came to a new country with nothing in our pocket. I felt very grateful for even the little that we did have.

Eating my first Big Mac I felt so grateful. I went to McDonald's for the first time in Marrickville, and people were just munching away like it was nothing special. But when I had my first Big Mac and vanilla milkshake, I just wanted to eat and drink really slowly so it didn't finish quickly! I was very grateful.

So perhaps try being a friend of poverty. It can help us to become grateful.

Giving up attachment

Is it helpful on the spiritual path to give up pleasures like a favourite food or affection for your family?

What we want to give up is not the outer, but the *inner* attachment.

If you eat junk food, but you're not attached to it, guess what? Sometimes it's not bad. I have to admit, occasionally I'll have some French fries from McDonald's if a friend buys them—very rarely!—just a few. That's nice. But I'm not attached to that.

So therefore if I don't see French fries for the next hundred years, it won't do anything to me. There's no salivating, there's no protest, there's no feeling upset, there's no withdrawal symptoms. Nothing.

So it's the attachment—the feeling that 'I *must* have it'—that's what you want to get rid of.

Being affectionate with your family is beautiful. Why would you stop loving another person? Is your family different? Why wouldn't you love your family? If you don't love your family, who can you love? They brought you into this world, they shared the journey with you.

But get rid of the idea that 'I must be with my family all the time' or 'I need to be with my family'. Get rid of the *attachment* to being with them, not the *actual* being with them.

When you don't have that attachment, then when you're with them you feel very free. And when you're away from them, you still feel very free. But when you have this 'I must' be with a person, then when you're not with them you'll feel disturbed.

So it's not the actual outer circumstance we want to change. We want to change the neurotic conditioning of I *must* have it—I *must* have delicious food, I *must* have affection. Because with that conditioning, when you don't have that thing, you're in trouble.

When I was growing up, until I started to have relationships in my life, I didn't really know what affection was. The most affection my father ever gave me was patting me on my head maybe once or twice in my whole life.

I missed that affection. But it was the idea that I *need* affection—the idea of it—which created corresponding neediness and suffering in my life. And when I got rid of that idea, then I had no problems.

So suffering is just caused by the idea that you need something, and you *must* have it.

There are no bad people

Is there such a thing as a bad person?

A bad person only exists in our mind. Outside that, there's no such thing as a bad person.

When you don't like another person, you think *they* are 'bad'. When the other person doesn't like you, in their eyes, in their mind, *you* are 'bad'. But you probably won't see yourself as bad.

It's like a person robs a bank, so we call them a criminal, but they don't see themself as a criminal. They just see themself as a nice person. They don't tell their children, "I am a criminal." They tell their children, "I am a loving father. I love you." They'll be kissing their child before they go to bed. They don't see themself as bad.

So there's no such thing as a bad person. That only exists in our mind, as a label about a person.

There *is* such a thing as a forgetful person—the person that forgot that they are the embodiment of love, so they express themself in a non-loving way. But there's no 'bad'.

'Good' and 'bad' only exist in a person's mind! And we believe the mind, that's all.

Cultivating kindness

At heart I feel like I am a good, kind, loving person. So why is my mind full of self-pity, resistance and judgement?

It's true—we are kind, loving people at heart. But most of us act that way only sometimes. We're kind and loving sometimes, but snapping or rude at other times. So that means our kindness and lovingness is not total. That's very different to someone who's kind and loving on a full-time basis, in what they think, say and do in every moment.

If we're just being kind and loving in a casual way—here and there, here and there—we don't see all the missed opportunities. We don't see all those times where we are not kind and loving— we're nasty, angry, jealous, and the rest. And when the kindness and lovingness is not total, there's room for negativity to come in and cause suffering in our life.

So partial kind-heartedness is better than zero kind-heartedness, but we should use that as a foundation to work towards making our kindness and lovingness become full-time.

Honouring your parents

Why is it so important to honour your mother and father—it seems like some parents are dreadful role models.

Our parents truly are our first gurus because they're the first people we set eyes on, really. They're the people that teach us how to walk, they're the people that teach us how to survive in the world, they're the people who feed us, they're the people who sacrifice their life for us.

So those people who feed you, love you, sacrifice their life for you—if you don't honour them, how are you going to be grateful towards others?

We should be grateful towards our parents for the beautiful qualities and for the negative qualities as well. Every person has strengths and weaknesses. Our parents are the same.

So the question is asking—can all parents be good role models? Absolutely. We learn so many good things from our parents. And we learn so many bad things from our parents! Both. And it's not our parents' fault. It's we who are not equipped to understand the art of how to get the gold and leave the dirt.

If a person is panning for gold, they're not going to take the dirt home with them. They'll take the panning equipment and the bits of gold and leave the dirt.

In the same way, we should be open and be grateful for our parents' great qualities. And for those so-called 'bad qualities' or 'negative qualities', we should also be grateful. We should be grateful because we can learn what *not* to be like, or what's not beneficial.

For example, say your father is angry and you pick up that habit. Well, you can decide that's not the way to be. You can learn how to stop that in you. When you're young maybe you can't help it—it just goes into you—but as soon as you have the maturity to understand, then you can learn how to stop it. That's a good thing.

Our parents are truly our first gurus, so we should love them and stop blaming them for things. Instead we should be so grateful for their contribution to our life.

Prayer

Does praying for someone actually make a difference for them?

It does! But much better than praying for someone is to help someone. One Master said beautifully, "Helping hands have more value than folded hands."

If I've got no food and I'm starving, and you've got plenty of food in your fridge at home, you can pray and pray and pray—and if you pray well enough maybe someone else will pick up that vibration and pop by and give me some food. But it's much quicker for you to just get some food out of your fridge and bring it over to me!

So helping hands have much more value than folded hands, but praying for the benefit of others is the next best thing. So if you can't help someone who's starving, then at least pray for them—"Oh God, the people are starving. I can't bear to see them starving. Please give them some food so they are able to live. Please God, help them." That's very powerful.

I don't know many formal prayers so I'm just making the prayer up, but God understands. God understands when I make a prayer like that because I mean it. I'm no prayer expert, but because I mean it God receives the text message straight away—there's no network breakdown or loss of signal. Immediately, it will be received.

But there are so many other ways to serve and help those in need, those who are suffering. Hear their story, hear from your heart.

Even sometimes when you don't do anything you are helping. For example, if somebody screams at you and you're just calm—you have no attacking thoughts towards them, you're not judging them, you're just peaceful and calm—believe it or not, that really helps them. It's not easy to do nothing in that moment—you probably want to throw your bag at them—but staying calm and not reacting is actually the best gift you can give that person in that moment.

Ultimately when we pray for others, we are sending our blessing to them. And because we are truly divine—even if we have forgotten that we are divine—our good thoughts for others, our good intentions, our love for others, is amazingly powerful. You can protect others—your loved ones—just by your love for them.

So prayer helps. It helps others, and in the process of helping others you awaken your divine nature and the infinite love that you truly are. In that sense, you're also helping yourself.

You should use prayer more often. You don't have to know how to pray. Just share your heart's wish, that's the best prayer. God will always hear that.

Feelings of guilt

I was raised to be kind and good, and I strive to be that way. So when I find myself doing things that aren't kind and good, I feel so guilty and ashamed. Could you talk about that?

We should always strive to be kind and good and compassionate. Why? Because that's our nature. It's like the nature of the sun is to shine, the nature of the river is to flow, the nature of the dog is to bark.

Our divine Self, our true nature, is to love, to be kind, to be good, to be compassionate, to have understanding for every being. So we should strive to express more of our nature. Why? Because that'll make us happy and we will also have better health.

Now, when we're not kind, when we're angry with other people, or we think badly of people or don't trust people, that's fine. Just know that's not you. That's the mind doing its job. That's the mind's job description. It's doing its thing. The nature of the mind is to divide and disturb, which can cause you to feel guilty. It's just doing its thing.

So when you're not kind, it's not really you, it's actually your mind. And if it's not you, what should you do? You should let it go—don't give it much thought.

For example, let's say you're in the same class as Tony in Year 6 at school, and Tony gets angry and throws a chair across the room, so he gets in big trouble.

Now, when Tony gets in trouble, do you feel guilty? You're just being quiet doing your spelling sheets, and Tony gets in big trouble. The teacher rings up his parents and suspends him from school. Do you feel guilty about Tony? You don't.

You know why? Because it's not you—you didn't do it. You weren't the one that threw the chair across the room, it was Tony. So you don't feel guilty.

In the same way, when the mind causes you to feel guilty, you should see it like that—know it's not you that got angry or was unkind, and don't give it much thought.

This perspective will help you to be more at peace with yourself and to overcome negative feelings such as guilt.

Maintaining calm in busyness

Sometimes I have so much to get done—I'm busy and I get caught up in getting the tasks done, and I completely lose the mindset to relax and feel peaceful through it all. How can I overcome that?

We have to learn and practise how to be present and how to be aware, so that when we're present, we *know* we're present. We have to be able to do that.

Now, if we are not able to do that, then we will live our life based on intervals of time. When we're at work, our interval will be the start and end of the shift. Or if you're a manager and you're interviewing someone for a job, you'll think, "I've got half an hour to interview this person."

You start to see your life as a series of intervals. So when a person gets overwhelmed and gets very busy, that means they have lots of intervals to squeeze into one day. Then they'll feel like they're rushing around under pressure.

But the reality is there's no such thing as intervals. Intervals are man-made. Time is man-made. To demonstrate that time is man-made—why do we have a leap year every four years? Because there are 60 seconds in a minute, 60 minutes in an hour, 24 hours in a day, 365 days in a year—and a little bit extra! They couldn't divide it perfectly, so every four years they fix up their error, and they call it a leap year. So the clock—the time we run our life by—is man-made.

Now, of course where there are intervals there are deadlines. And when we have too many deadlines it'll make us sick. Why does it make us sick? Because it's unnatural. It's artificial. It's not real. It's like eating food which is full of preservatives—it will make you sick.

So learn how to be present. Because when you are present there are no deadlines. Or you can say you're pretending there are deadlines, but deep down you know there aren't any.

Then, if you go for a job interview and they say, "We'll let you know the outcome in a few days"—you won't get nervous, with sweaty palms and sleepless nights, waiting. Because you know there's no such thing as an interval of three days. There's just this moment, the eternal now. You don't live your life in time intervals like that.

So how does it look when a person is heaps busy but they live in the present moment? Well, I'll tell you how it looks. It looks like they're engaged in all sorts of things, no different to anybody else. Their body might be moving fast if they are running late for a meeting, but inside them there's no rush, there's absolute calm.

What makes them different from other people is there's no pressure in their mind, there's no deadline. So they don't feel flat, they don't drain their energy, they don't worry, they don't think. They just live in the moment. And when they live in the present moment, there's always love and enjoyment.

In sports, when you're able to be present they say you 'stretch out time'. When a cricket batsman is concentrating on a ball coming at 140 km/hr from the bowler, he only has a split second before the ball reaches him. But a batsman who is fully present can stretch it out so it appears to him like more than one second—he sees the ball come off the bowler's hand, he sees the seam of the ball, and he sees the twist of the ball every moment in the air as it approaches him. Everything seems so slow to him, so he is giving himself more time to respond.

So learn how to be present. Don't let 'the present moment' remain just a few words and theories. Learn how to apply the present moment in your life. Then your life will feel like you have all the time in the world. Your life will feel like an eternal joy.

Hope for the world

Is there any hope for this world?

If we all individually try our best to have some peace in our life, then there's lots of hope for the world.

Let's use an example of a house—a five bedroom house with ten people living there whose minds are not in peace but in pieces. Now, if the house is a symbol of the world then there's not much hope. If one person forgets to put the toilet lid down or something, there will be riots!

But if each of the ten people has a certain level of peacefulness and calmness, then there's hope for the house. There's hope that they can live together in harmony. If one person forgets to put the toilet lid down the other nine will have the patience to encourage the person! And the one that forgets to put the toilet lid down has the peacefulness and calmness to be open for change, for the sake of the harmony of the other nine.

So we can't just say whether there's hope for the world. We have to ask how peaceful the individuals on this planet are, then that will determine the hope for the planet.

How can we contribute to world peace?

By having peace within us. World peace begins with individual peace.

We have to ask ourself—what does world peace mean? World peace means peace on planet Earth. And what makes planet Earth not peaceful? Human beings. Not nature, not animals— human beings. The disorderliness, the destruction of this planet, is caused by human beings.

And what makes up the human race? Individuals. There are seven billion individuals on the planet, starting off with the family unit, and then the community, and then the region, state, country and planet.

When each individual has that inner peace, then world peace will be automatic. Because if everybody has that inner peace,

47

nobody will want to fight another person, nobody will want to hurt another person—their actions will come out of peace.

We should always ask ourself—if the whole planet was made up of me, seven billion copies of me, what would the planet look like? Would it be a world at peace or would it be a world in pieces? We should ask ourself that question.

That's the formula for world peace. It starts with the inner peace of one individual.

Experiences during meditation

Often when I meditate, my spine suddenly snaps upright and I go very still. What is happening?

There's something funny happening.

You see, meditation is a state of deep calmness, stillness of energy, and peace. It is a deep relaxation, a soul restfulness. That's the meditation state.

Now, if your spine snaps up or snaps left or snaps right or snaps back, that doesn't sound like deep relaxation. That must be something else.

Somebody said to a Master, "Guruji, I've been meditating for 20 years and nothing has happened. Nothing." And the Guru said, "You should be thankful nothing happened! You should feel blessed that nothing happened to you in 20 years."

When we're meditating, we tend to want something to happen. We want to see some bright light, we want some sort of tingling sensation in our spine or we want our spine to snap upright—we want something to happen.

Why do we want something like this to happen? There must be some sort of motive. It could be that if something happens—something visual or something physical—that shows that our meditation is working. We think it's a sign.

It's like if somebody buys the drug ecstasy and nothing happens when they take it, so they'll say, "Nothing happened, I got ripped off." But if your goal is for nothing to happen, then something happened. That nothing is something.

So it depends on what your goal is. If your goal is for nothing to happen and then suddenly your spine snaps forward or back, what are you going to think of that? If you're a good meditator you're going to think, "That wasn't it. That was *something*. I'm looking for *nothing*."

If you continue looking for nothing, then nothing will happen. And when nothing happens in your life, you will become the embodiment of emptiness. You'll become a Buddha.

The role of animals

Could you talk about animals and what role they have in the world and with humans?

Animals are very happy and human beings are not very happy, so if we hang around animals, that helps us to become happy. The animals came to this planet to do this job—to make us happy. We are so fortunate to have animals on this planet.

So if you happen to be feeling unhappy in your life, give yourself a gift—let a pet be your friend. A cat or a dog—whatever you like as a pet. We can benefit so much from them.

We can learn a lot from animals. We think it's us taking care of them, but I'm not so sure who's taking care of who. We provide them with food and shelter, but they give us so much more—they give us great joy.

When you're feeling sad, which friend of yours is going to always be there for you? The animals will—cats and dogs and other pets will immediately pick up your low energy and they will help to uplift you. So we are indebted to the animals and we should be grateful and take care of them well.

Human beings cannot live happily on food and shelter alone—we need a minimum level of peacefulness, otherwise it's very hard to remain sane in this world. It's not a coincidence when we have a pet. That pet knew long ago before it came to this planet that it was coming to help us to be happy. I love animals, just on that fact alone.

So everybody should have a pet if they can, and we should at least give them good food and look after them. That's our minimum duty. And be their friend. Don't just get a pet and then leave it on its own all the time. They want to be close, they want to help, they want to make us happy. So the least we can do is let them do their job to make us happy.

Watching TV

Is watching TV OK?

TV is really a great invention, but it depends on what you're watching on TV. In the same way, books can be great, but it depends on what type of books you're reading. And friends can be great companions, but it depends on what type of friends you have!

So TV can be good—you can watch beautiful things that inspire your life. You can watch movies or documentaries that show people who are innocent, heroic, honest, courageous, honourable, peaceful and loving. To watch that on TV is very good.

I won't mention the things that we watch that are not good—I think we can guess that!

So watching TV can be good or bad—but it depends on what we're watching. We are like sponges—whatever we witness, we soak in, and that will become our experience. So if we witness violence all the time, we'll soak that in and then that will be our life experience.

So be careful what you witness. Try not to witness violence and hatred. Try to witness kindness and compassion and love in action. Try to witness people who are peaceful and selfless. Try to witness peaceful warriors, people who endeavour to conquer their own mind—not people who try to conquer other territories or people. Try to witness people who are true inner warriors. Try to witness saints, because that might become your experience one day. Watch documentaries or movies of saints like Amma, St Francis of Assisi, Dilgo Kyentse Rinpoche, the Dalai Lama and Meher Baba.

Overall, I think TV is very good, because I know what type of things I want to witness. But TV could be very harmful—it all depends on what you're witnessing.

Selfless giving

Giving some of your wealth to charity is said to benefit the receiver as well as the giver—is that true?

Yes—selflessness is beneficial for the recipient, and for the person who's actually being selfless. It benefits both.

Your heart might feel, "I haven't got time to go out and help people who are suffering, but I can give to someone who can." So then you donate some of your income to help those in need, and in that way you yourself are helping them.

It comes down to selflessness. Every problem in the world—mental illness and violence and crime and starvation—is caused by selfishness. But when you are selfless, what you're saying is, "I am nothing. The world, other people, God's creation, are everything." Once you have that feeling of nothingness in you, there's no ego left—and it's the ego that causes you feelings of suffering.

So selflessness is without a doubt a very powerful method to end suffering. It benefits you as well as the recipient. And giving your money to charity is one way to practice selflessness.

Jesus

What do you love about Jesus?

He had a passion that was immeasurable. Or you can call it a big heart—such a big heart to help others realise their godliness. His passion was like 1,000 suns burning. If you had a wish to realise your godliness, he'd do anything for you. That's the type of passion he had.

He never thought of anything for himself. He was just so loving.

And another thing that made Jesus so beautiful was he was such an ordinary person. He was born in a manger—no glitter thrown around and no balloon popping. Just such an ordinary person—on the outside. But on the inside, he had a heart that you couldn't find in a billion people. Such passion.

He is opposite to the world we live in. The world we live in is just plagued with selfishness, but he didn't have even one gram of selfishness in him. He'd climb mountains, he'd walk across water, he'd do anything to help someone realise their greatness, realise the God in them.

He was so true to himself and so charismatic—because charisma comes not from a skill, but from oozing confidence in the divine Self within. He was so charismatic, but at the same time he was so ordinary. And he wasn't shy to let people know his greatness so that they could see their own greatness. His philosophy was—'I will use anything that benefits the person and helps them remember who they truly are.'

He would say things like, "I am the life and the way. If you doubt there is a God or you find it difficult to connect with that formless God, then come through me, live with me and around me, and then you will see God, you will realise God." But he wasn't boasting, he said that just like a Vietnamese person eats rice for breakfast, lunch and dinner—like it's just normal.

Jesus was such a great friend. He was strict in some sense, but in another sense he was so easy-going. Let's put it this way—you'd feel very comfortable in his company, you wouldn't feel pressured. He'd give you space to do whatever you like.

He was very light. He would tell jokes and he wouldn't allow his disciples to take things too seriously. He'd always bring them back to simplicity.

And he was so loyal—someone it was impossible not to trust. It used to pain him when people didn't trust him. He'd feel, "Why? Why don't you trust? Why don't you have faith in me? Don't you understand how much more happy your life will be if you trust me—how great your life will be, if you have faith in me?"

Such a great Master he was. He had such a big heart—you couldn't have a bigger heart than Jesus. There have been Masters who have had an equally big heart, but none bigger than Jesus.

A lot of his teachings were shared just through spending time with him. Most of the disciples would just hang around him, and they'd help the poor and needy. He had a soft spot for the poor and needy. He wasn't a Master for only the poor—he was a Master for everyone, and he loved everyone. But he had a soft spot for the poor and needy, because they tend to have innocence together with their struggle. So he wanted to make them happy.

I have so much reverence for Jesus. He is my dear friend. Amongst Masters, he's one of the Masters I feel closest to. He helped me on my path tremendously. When I was living in the world and I had no Master, he was my Master. I used to have the book called *God Calling*, and in my times of need I would open the book and I'd read it. I read it a lot, and every time I read it, it would make me cry in comfort.

He has such a loving heart, he's a lover of nature and a lover of all. That's what I feel about Jesus.

Bhakti—the path of love

What is bhakti?

'Bhakti' means devotion or love towards a Master, towards God. It's a path towards enlightenment, a way to realise our true Self.

There are many paths towards enlightenment, but the path of love is probably the easiest.

It's like the jackfruit tree. What's interesting about a jackfruit tree is that it has fruits on the branches at the top of the trunk but it also has fruits right at the bottom of the trunk. You can have a jackfruit the size of a watermelon coming out of the trunk, and it's only a metre off the ground. So it has big fruits at the bottom, not just at the top.

In the same way, on the path of love you start to receive the fruits right at the beginning, when you first begin your journey— you will feel peaceful and sweet immediately.

On other paths it takes time—you get the fruits towards the end. But when you start the path of love, you're already getting some royalties at the beginning! And then you get a big payout at the end.

So why is that important? Why does that make the journey easier?

Because when we first start, in the beginning, we need encouragement. We need some evidence that it's working.

It's like a person starting to train as a body builder and they can see in the mirror, "Ah, I'm getting some muscles," so nobody needs to encourage them to go to the gym anymore—they'll be going automatically. If they take a break and then look in the mirror and their muscles are shrinking, they'll say, "Oops! I'm going to the gym to get the muscles back." So in the beginning it's the results that encourage us.

Then, as you get more and more results, you start to have more and more faith in the path. Then you become more focussed, more total. In time you become unwavering on the path towards the goal.

So the path of love, in that sense, is the easiest.

The ideal disciple

What does a Spiritual Master most hope for in a disciple?

Someone whose sincere and heartfelt wish is to be happy all the time. Then the Master's job is easier. If the Master is a tennis coach and the disciple loves golf, then it's very difficult to make that disciple into a really good tennis player.

It sounds simple, but it's not that simple! Because quite often the disciple wants to live a certain way—see things with a certain perspective, in the belief that it will make them happy. But it doesn't actually make them truly happy.

So when the disciple has the wish to be *truly* happy, then it makes the Master's job much easier.

Part 2

Practical Wisdom

"Strength comes from the love of oneself, the love of others, the love of the world and the love of God."

Being a householder

If someone hasn't chosen to live the life of a nun or a monk, what's the best way for them to live as a householder or a layperson?

To always have the goal in mind.

It doesn't matter if you're a monk or a nun or a householder, what matters is you always have the goal in mind—the goal of being peaceful and calm in every moment of your life.

As a householder, you will go towards the goal as long as you have that goal in mind. And a monk or nun will have that same goal—so aren't you really the same? One person is sitting calmly and peacefully in the monastery, and the other one is cooking calmly and peacefully at home for the family. So in terms of the goal of calmness and peacefulness, there's no difference.

The challenge to remain calm and peaceful is slightly different for a householder than for a monk or nun, but essentially it's the not that different.

The main challenge for a householder is that it can be more difficult to create a close connection with the Master. If you are living in a monastery or an ashram, you're right there with the Master, so it's easier to develop a relationship. It's generally more difficult to develop this connection if you're not seeing each other physically on some sort of regular basis.

So a householder has that disadvantage—they don't see the Master as often, so they're forced to connect with the Master from a distance.

When you're in a monastery or an ashram, it's a lot easier to think of the goal, to focus on the goal, to focus on God. However when you're a householder, to do this is a lot more challenging because you're distracted more easily.

In a monastic environment it is easier to focus because you have less on your plate, less distraction—you've got your routine, your life is quite simple, there's no worry about how to earn an income, how to put food on the table. It's more simplified.

But if a householder has the goal in mind, even though it's more challenging, it's possible for them to achieve peacefulness and calmness in all situations in life.

When I was a seeker, I always thought, "If there is one person on the planet that has achieved the goal, why can't I?" So in that case, a householder would think, "Are there any householders that have achieved the goal? And if they have, then why can't I?" And the answer is 'Yes'. There have been many householders on the planet who attained enlightenment. So it is possible for anyone who truly commits to the goal.

Now, if I'm 4ft tall and I want to play basketball in the NBA league in America, it doesn't matter how strong my wish is, how focussed I am, how much I practise basketball—I will not be able to play for the NBA. So there are limitations there. But a life of peacefulness and calmness is one goal that anyone can achieve. We are our only limitation, and the limitation is that we don't have that goal as first priority in our life.

So it doesn't matter if you're a householder or not. What's important is you have the goal sincerely in your heart.

Relationships

How can I give my relationship the best chance of success?

What destroys a relationship the most is when we hurt another person's feelings. Nobody wants their feelings to be hurt, so if you hurt someone's feelings they'll want to leave you.

So every time you hurt someone, no matter what causes you to do that, the other person feels the blow of it, the impact. And every time we hurt someone's feelings in a relationship, the person will get their mental diary out and write, "It's happened again. I'll endure a few more times, and after that—see you later!"

So what you want to do is be peaceful, not reactive. If someone causes you anger, don't get angry back. Be peaceful. If you want to destroy a relationship, the fastest way is to get angry at someone.

When we're very peaceful, people love us, they are not afraid of us. That creates beautiful relationships. There's more closeness, there's more friendship, there's no fear. You don't feel like the person comes in the room and takes over your space. You don't feel, "Oh, I need a break from this!" You feel a natural comfortable closeness. It's a joy to be together, like two birds flying together in the sky.

So the main thing in relationships is to be peaceful. Be proactive in practicing peacefulness.

How do we know when we should leave an unhappy relationship or when we should stay in the relationship and try to become happy in it?

Sometimes when we want to leave someone, we can't leave—we're too attached to that person. And other times when we don't want to leave them, we end up becoming separated anyway!

So a lot of it is outside our hands. It's like when I used to get on the roller coaster at Australia's Wonderland—once it goes, you just can't get off. It has its own journey. And a person might have a roller coaster ride with somebody for three months, or three years, or 30 years. Then that's it.

If a couple has been in a relationship for 50 years, it looks like a great success. But you don't know how many times they might have tried to leave each other in that 50 years. Maybe multiple times. They tried, but for some reason they just couldn't do it. And if they did finally leave each other, they might have felt, "Why didn't I do that ages ago? Why did I wait so long?"

So a lot of times it's not what we want, it's just destiny. Just go with the flow. And try not to focus on the physical outcome too much, but try to change your perspective, your attitude, during the relationship. And when the time is naturally up, life will make you move on.

Friendship

What's the best way to develop good friendships?

Be yourself. That's how I developed beautiful friendships.

I wouldn't have a clue how to make friends with someone, or what technique to use—and I've read the book, *How to Win Friends and Influence People!* I've still got absolutely no clue how to develop friendships. Or influence people!

As a matter of fact, I'm terrible at influencing people. All I know is I'm just being myself, and if a person is influenced or not, that's outside my hands. I'm certainly not trying to influence anybody, because if I try to influence them they might feel I'm trying to convert them to something. Influencing others doesn't work. So why bother?

Being yourself is so beautiful. You just know how to respond. You know how to develop friendships. How do you know? Because you are the dearest of friends, by your nature. You are ancient, you've developed friendships for millions of years. You do know how. You don't need to be taught or to read books about how to win friends. Why would you need books like that? You already know how.

The next thing is, friends are picked by God, not by us. How do you look for friends? Which pub do you go to? Which shopping centre do you hang around? Which beach do you swim at? Where do you go to find a friend?

If you look at your life, all your dearest friends came into your life without any effort. Sometimes it's a friend's friend— it just happens naturally. A person helps you with something, and you connect—and then suddenly you're friends. I'm talking about your dear friends. On this planet we meet thousands and thousands of people, but very few become your dear friends.

You have to understand that you can't *find* friends, so there's no point trying. Just be yourself, and suddenly friendship happens naturally.

If we look at our planet today there's so much loneliness. We're just not good at making beautiful friends. Guess why? Because we're not good at being ourselves. So be yourself.

Now, if for some reason you are being yourself and you still haven't met any good, dear friends yet, then let God be your friend. Speak to God. Be that brave weirdo that speaks to God. If you think God can't hear you, just pretend God hears you— because God *does* hear you.

It doesn't mean you can't have other friends when you have a friendship with God.

I've always been a shy person in social situations, but God brought me dear friends. When I was in Amma's ashram, and travelling with Amma for three and a half years, I was shy. In the Western canteen, people were eating and sitting and talking together—and I used to sit there like a dork, not knowing what to say! I didn't know how to socialise. I was awkward. So I used to like going to the Indian section where no-one knew me! I'd just eat on the table among the Indians—we didn't know each other, so then I didn't feel any awkwardness.

And even though I was shy like that, I made dear friends. At my first big program on tour with Amma, I was the pot washer. I went there by myself from Australia and I didn't know one person.

There were 120,000 people at the program and the rice team was cooking rice to feed the big crowd. The team was so busy shovelling the rice, drying the rice out, and dumping it in an area to get ready to feed the people for dinner. It looked like they were struggling and couldn't keep up with the rice cooking.

There was no-one else washing the pots—I was the only one that showed up to the assigned duty! I said, "Have I come to the wrong place?" They said, "No, no, that's pot washing."

So because there was nobody else around, I had to wash the pots very quickly. I just dived in—I saw it as a great opportunity and I washed pots wholeheartedly.

A German devotee there saw me pot-washing and he said to me, "You can stop pot-washing and come and help cook the rice." I asked, "Am I allowed?" He said, "Yes, you're allowed!" So I started cooking rice and then he said, "You stay with the rice cooking now."

His name was Krishna, and he became my dear friend on tour. He'd been there for four or five years so he showed me the ropes. He showed me where to buy beautiful lassi drinks! He showed me everything. He made it easy.

After that, I cooked rice on every Indian tour. We hung around together and we were great friends. We shared everything, including our hearts and our feelings. You can't go out and find a friend like that.

And then I met another good friend when I was supervising the veggie chopping in the kitchen at Amritapuri, Amma's ashram. The shift finished but we hadn't finished all the work so I was still veggie chopping after everyone left, and this one Spanish guy was still there—his name was David but I called him Amigo.

I said to Amigo, "The shift is finished so if you need to go you can." He said, "No, no, I'd like to stay and help." So he stayed helping me and we started cracking jokes and we became great friends.

So God will find you your friends. God knows how to do it. All you have to do is be yourself, and dear friends will come.

Losing a loved one

How would you recommend living with the loss of a loved one who passed away suddenly and tragically in an accident?

The truth is, life is very hard. We have to be honest with ourselves—living on this planet is a challenge, it's not easy.

My life hasn't been easy. When I was three my mother died in an accident. My father was a deep-sea fisherman—he'd go to the ocean for five weeks and then come back to spend one week with the family, and then go off again for four or five weeks. So I didn't have a mother, and I saw my father for about 10 weeks a year. Life was hard.

So life can be very hard, and the death of your dearest friend or a loved one is one example of that.

If we live on this planet and we don't live close to our spirit, it's very hard to survive. There's so much loneliness. It breaks my heart just to see so many people living with loneliness.

If we don't know our spirit, we're in trouble. But when you know your spirit and the nature of spirit, then life won't be so harsh. How could that be? What can the spirit do to make life less harsh? It can understand the bigger picture. It can see perfection in everything. It can see that life never ends. It can see that death is just one holiday ending, preparing for the next holiday to begin. The soul just knows that.

So, when a person passes away, I would say mourn for the person. Not out of a rule, but as a way to show your love and honouring of that spirit that was in the body. It's kind of like respect, because respect comes from love.

So we can mourn for some time. It's an opportunity to express our love again. In some ways mourning for a friend is a greater opportunity than when the friend was alive, because sometimes if a friend is alive we take them for granted. But when the friend leaves, it's a great opportunity to love the person, to express our love.

So take time to mourn for your friend or your family or your dear one—not like death is a bad thing, but as an opportunity to cherish your beautiful memories of them.

Overcoming depression

How can a person overcome depression?

There's only one way to overcome depression, and that relates to the cause of depression—how it actually works.

The cause of depression is when our vitality or our energy is flat. So the next question is—how did that energy go flat?

I'll explain with an example. We've got about 40,000 litres of water in our rainwater tanks here at the ashram, so imagine one day we turn on the tap but no water comes out. Then we go down underneath the house and have a look in the tanks, and we find there's no water left. If the tanks were full two days ago, how could they be empty now? The water must have been running out—someone left a tap on!

So when someone has depression, that means they left the tap on and there's just no vitality left. I wouldn't say zero vitality left, because zero vitality means your body will be like a log— you'll be dead. But when you hit a certain level of low vitality, you'll be depressed.

So how do you fix the problem? If you left the tap on, what do you do? You pray for rain, and you walk around to check that every tap is firmly closed. And when the rain comes, if there's no leakage from the taps, the water tanks will slowly become full.

I'm using water as a metaphor here, but vitality is similar to this. So how does that vitality leak out? It leaks out through thoughts.

Now, it doesn't matter whether you leave your tap on purposefully or you just forget—the water will still run out. In the same way, it doesn't matter if you are aware that you're constantly thinking, or if you're just thinking all the time and you're not aware of it. Both will leak vitality and drain your energy.

Our maximum vitality cannot be measured in 40,000 litre tanks—it is tremendously more. It is millions of litres! And we are constantly thinking—thinking this, thinking that, solving this, planning that. All day we're thinking, so our energy is leaking constantly.

But we don't get flat in one or two years. It'll take at least a decade. A newborn baby has an absolutely full tank. And for a newborn to get to twenty something years or thirty something years, and then be flat, you can see it took a long time to think their way to depression.

So how do you stop depression? You close all the taps so there's no leakage. That means you have to know how to control your thoughts and your mind.

Breath meditation

What are the key things I need to know about breath meditation?

Focus your attention and awareness on the breath. That's one of the best techniques, because the breath is always with you.

If you love roses and you focus on roses as a form of meditation to bring you to the present moment, what happens if someone screams at you and there are no roses around? Do you run to the florist shop straight away to calm yourself down?

So the breath is always with you. When someone upsets you, you can focus on your breath straight away—slowly breathe in, slowly breathe out. By focusing that way, your mind doesn't go off into your thoughts, your conditioning.

That's called mastering the mind—when you don't allow your mind to take you away into your thoughts. When the mind takes you away that's like the tail wagging the dog.

When you're able to concentrate on your breath and then just remain there as long as you like—while you're washing the dishes, while you're sitting on the toilet, while you're walking, while you're eating, whatever you're doing—that means the dog is wagging the tail. You should aim to achieve that.

But you have to practise.

So breath meditation is one form of meditation. There are many other practices that are just as great, but breath meditation is probably one of the most commonly practised, just purely because the breath is always with us.

Anger

What advice can you give me in a situation where my anger takes over me?

Try your best to calm down, because when you get angry the anger creates a chemical in your body that eats away at you, causing ulcers and diseases.

It not only causes this type of physical destruction for yourself, but it causes suffering for other people as well.

So have the understanding that your anger is harming others and yourself.

Having that understanding, just try your best to calm down as much as you can in that moment, and make a vow to never do that towards another person again.

Now, I think we all understand that prevention is the best medicine. So it's good to train your mind so that you are able to control your thoughts and your emotions when you want to.

So if you understand life and you know you're going to go through circumstances where, because of your conditioning, you're going to have explosions of anger, you should train or practise ahead of time to prevent that.

You do spiritual practice to purify and clear your conditioning, and you practise self-control in moments in your life when you struggle to handle your anger. That failure is actually not a failure—you can use it to prepare for the next opportunity. And then you get better and better at it, until you are in a situation that normally makes you angry, but you're able to be calm.

So as a preventative, you can train ahead like this, thinking like an Olympian—"In four years time, I'm going to go to the

Olympics. So I'll start training now." But if a person hasn't trained and they just rock up to the Olympics, what advice can you give them? I guess that they just try their best. That's all they can do. But they're not going to perform very well.

So they are the two scenarios. Practise ahead, as a preventative, or just try your best in the moment.

But if I try not to get angry at someone, isn't that just suppression, which will explode some other time?

The scenario that we understand as 'suppression' is when somebody gets angry and they don't say anything on the outside, but they're fuming inside, and they go home and explode towards their family.

But what I'm talking about is not that scenario. What I'm talking about is controlling the cause of the anger—the thoughts. Switch off the thoughts so there are no corresponding emotions of anger arising.

Emotions will always follow thoughts like a shadow, so if there are no thoughts happening, then anger cannot arise. This is the key factor.

If we are not aware of the thoughts that are coming in that moment, then they happen automatically so we have no control over them. But if you are aware of your thoughts and therefore you are able to control them, then there'll be no anger arising inside you.

Loving versus being loved

There's a prayer from St Francis that says, 'Grant that I may seek not to be understood or to be loved, but to love and to understand.' But so often we seek love and understanding first. Could you talk about how we can let go of seeking to be loved and understood, and to focus only on loving and understanding others?

The wanting others to love us and the wanting others to understand us is not based on truth. Because we are naturally the embodiment of love and wisdom. That's our nature. So when we look to others to give us love and understanding, that means we have forgotten that we are that mansion of love and wisdom.

So we shouldn't be seeking to receive love and understanding. Instead, we should try to realise our true Self so that we can experience the love and wisdom that we are.

The more we realise our true Self, the more we will be able to understand ourself and the world. We'll be able to love infinitely, without running out. How can you run out of love? You can run out of fuel, but love never runs out.

When we seek for others to love us and we seek for others to understand us, immediately we're telling ourself that we lack those things—that we don't have love and understanding—which is false.

So by our nature, we shouldn't seek for others to love us and to understand us. We should just express our love to others and try to be open, be curious, to understand others and to feel other people's feelings, their suffering and their joy. That's the way to happiness.

Loneliness

We all feel lonely from time to time. What actions can we take to be free of that feeling?

Loneliness is the feeling that you haven't got support. The feeling that no-one loves you. The feeling that when you need help, there's no-one around.

But you see, that's not true—there are always loved ones and friends, and there are always communities and Masters, who are there for us and who love us.

So these loneliness feelings are not true. There's an error. It's an error of the mind. An error caused by separation. We separate ourself from our family, we separate ourself from society, we separate ourself from everybody. And then we feel lonely. So the issue is really about separation and division, or oneness and connectedness.

Now, if you feel lonely and you try to go where the big crowds are, that's not going to fix it. Because it's not a physical issue—it's a psychological issue, you see. When you're separating yourself from the world, you're doing it psychologically.

So to overcome loneliness, the solution is to not separate yourself psychologically. Then you will start to experience oneness or connection. Suddenly you will love your family. And you will feel that your family, your friends, your pets, love you.

How do we separate ourself from others, from the world, and end up feeling unloved? By our thought that no-one loves us, that's how. But it's just a thought!

I'd like to ask a question. Why is it, if a person feels lonely and they don't feel loved, that they only feel that sometimes?

If it's true that no-one loves you, you should be lonely every moment of your life. You said nobody loves you. It should be every moment, every day, every year! Why is it sometimes you feel love and other times not?

The reason you feel lonely in those moments is because you have a thought that triggers a feeling of loneliness. So control that thought, or switch off that thought, then loneliness will be gone.

Develop the ability to control your mind and loneliness will be forever gone.

Nagging parents

My parents are continually finding fault with me, which just pushes my buttons and then I react in anger. Can you suggest how I can stay loving instead of reacting?

We should have the attitude that when somebody suggests something to us, we receive that just as information. Now it's up to us to take on the information and apply it in our life, or to discard it.

Not just with parents, but everybody. When someone gives you a suggestion, in whatever way—even if they're trying to influence or pressure you—it still comes down to the fact that it's just words.

So it is up to us to learn how to be detached from the pressure of the situation and objectively assess it. Is the suggestion they made like the crunchy sweet part of an apple which we choose to eat, or is it like the wormy part of the apple that we choose to slice off and put in the compost bin?

We should see our parents' suggestions like that. It should not be anything more than that, besides feeling grateful that our parents share their thoughts with us.

We should not blame our parents when they are pressing our buttons. We should admire their qualities of willpower and persistence, and we should learn how to be persistent and have endurance like them. And notice the strength in them too. We can learn from those qualities, but apply them in a different way in our life.

Because our parents love us so much, they want the best for us. Whatever they are suggesting, their intention is sponsored by love, and it's important that we try to understand that.

Now in the rare circumstance that we happen to be more wise than our parents, then with that wisdom we should respond accordingly—with patience, with understanding, with love, with gratitude.

How best to serve children

What's the best thing that we can do for the children in our lives?

Gandhi said beautifully, "Be the change you want to see." Whatever you want to see in your children, you be that.

You should be a good example because children are the best at copying. A child's job description is, 'I will copy, no matter what'. If there's a Guinness Book record for the best copier, I bet you that will be a child, not an adult.

So the question is, what will the child copy? Whichever way you are, they'll learn and become that.

If you want your children to be strong, not influenced by the negativities and harm and suffering of this world, then you should be an example of that. You should be strong, you should be courageous, you should be loving, you should be unshakeable, you should have faith. If you want your children to be wise and happy, you should be wise and happy. Then the rest is up to them.

So be a great example. Don't teach your children just by words—"Be nice, be kind."—and then treat other people with rudeness and frustration. The child won't learn from the words— they will absorb what they see and they'll copy that.

So it's up to us. It's up to the adults to be an example—to be a suffering example or to be a beautiful example. The child will copy either. The child won't even judge the difference. They'll just copy what they see, and become like that.

Managing responsibilities

I have so many responsibilities at work and at home and I feel like I'm drowning. I don't feel I can reduce my responsibilities, so how can I cope?

It's a certain way of looking at our life that makes us feel this responsibility, this heavy burden. It's a perspective.

So if we feel this heavy burden because we've been looking at life in that way, nothing will change until we change the way we look at our life. We have to shift the way we look at our life to a totally different angle, a different perspective.

I always say we did not come to this planet to complete a long list of tasks and then die. If you have that type of mindset, you have a lot of responsibility.

We came to this planet as a soul, jumping in this vehicle called the body, to just experience the magnificence of God's creation.

Always know that you are the invincible soul, the driver.

We did not come here to have a competition where whoever takes on the most responsibility on the planet wins the gold medal!

So we need a totally different mindset.

And if we can dig ourself into a hole by having a certain perspective on life, know that we can dig ourself out of the hole just by seeing life with a new perspective. If there's a way in, there's a way out.

It may be challenging, but it all depends on the attitude we adopt.

How to help a friend with addictions

My friend is falling back into drugs and alcohol. How can I help him?

You help him by not changing him, but by loving him. By being your Self, your divine Self. By being peaceful, by being joyful, by being happy. Just being your Self, your true Self—without the drugs.

And your friend will catch on to that. Your friend will be naturally curious about you, wondering how you are being an absolute joy to be with, but you're not taking drugs. Then they'll feel, "I don't need drugs either." And suddenly they have the determination and willpower to flick it.

So you have to be happy, you have to be joyful, you have to vibrate that.

If you are miserable and you don't take drugs, the friend will feel, "Well, you're the same as me so I'll just continue taking drugs." They're not going to believe whatever you say to try to help them.

So it comes down to your own joyfulness. When you take delight in yourself, the person will feel, "I want to be myself like that, and that's for free. This drug thing costs a lot and it causes me side effects. Whatever divine drug you're taking, it's for free and there are no side-effects—I'll have one of those please."

That's how you help your friend.

Overcoming fear

What is fear and how can we overcome it?

Fear is the opposite of love. Like light is the opposite of darkness.

When the light increases, darkness will decrease. So when love increases, fear will decrease.

What is fear? Fear is this thing that tenses you up. You tense up, you contract.

When a person has fear of public speaking, they contract. When a person is fearful of a situation, their voice will go a bit funny because they're not relaxed—their muscles contract and they can't speak properly.

Fear is who you are not. Who you are is love. So to get rid of fear, you have to cultivate love. To cultivate love, love people, be kind to people. Try your best to do that. Try your best with that intention, with that purpose.

And slowly, over time, you will conquer your fear. Then in the challenging situations in life where fear would arise, you'll be relaxed in love instead of contracting in fear.

Peace

There's so much suffering in the world from wars and fighting. What's the best way that we can help?

Be peaceful. Know that there's only one sun shining on this planet, but that one sun benefits so many—millions and millions.

When you shine your true spirit beautifully like the sun— bright and clear—then you'll be amazed how the contribution of just one person can affect the world. You'll be amazed how much peacefulness one person can contribute to the world.

And if every single person strives to shine their light like that—not dwelling in negativity, but shining their true colours— then the impact on world peace will be immeasurable.

When that happens it will go beyond the point where there is no war—because even if there's no war, that doesn't mean there's love. It will move to the point where humans on this planet will love each other, will be kind to each other and will help each other.

So if we each gain victory over our inner war of anger and hatred and other negative emotions, this will put an end to war. Then there will be world peace.

You've spoken about how being peaceful can help the suffering of people in the world. What about nature—what are a few things we can do to help the natural environment?

When we are peaceful, this state of peacefulness naturally wants to express itself.

Once a person is peaceful, everything that comes out of them has an impact of peacefulness—the look in their eyes, the words they speak, the wish in their heart, the vibration they project—everything about them will contribute to peace.

If they're walking in the garden the plants feel very peaceful, the plants feel very happy. If they're swimming in the river, the river feels, "Wow, what a delight to have this person swim here." When you go for a walk in the morning, and the sun rises, the sun is excited just to touch its light on you.

Everything in nature will adore you. Even an ant. When you're looking at an ant it will feel you love it. The ant will feel peaceful. The ant will know you won't hurt it. The ant will look at you with curiosity, but it will know you won't hurt it. It will know you love it.

Everything in nature will benefit when you are being peaceful. Everything will feel the impact of your peace.

If we are all peaceful—if we have that inner calm, that inner peace—then nature will be celebrating. Nobody will pollute the rivers, nobody will cause destruction to Mother Earth—because those actions that cause destruction are sponsored by lack of peacefulness. In this way nature will benefit from our peacefulness.

It's said that we should try to maintain our inner peace and inner silence regardless of whatever activity is happening around us. So is there any benefit in choosing lifestyles and professions that are less stressful, if the goal is to maintain that inner calm only?

Yes. For example, let's say you're in primary school and you've just learned how to swim. You can swim ten metres across the width of the pool, but you haven't got the strength to swim the length yet. Now, does it make sense to go to Bondi Beach and start surfing the waves? No. You can drown.

In the same way, in the beginning when we're learning how to still our energy and be calm within us, we should strive not to put ourselves in very extreme and difficult situations, where we start to drown emotionally. Because we're still just learning.

But when we get better and better, and we become a very good swimmer, then we should go to the beach and catch waves, because that makes us an even better swimmer. Those big waves come and hit us, and that is actually good for our swimming skills. Because that makes us gain experience, that makes us gain more confidence in swimming.

Then when the tsunami comes, we have a slightly better chance! If you can only swim the width of the pool, when the tsunami comes you've got no chance.

So in that sense it's good in the beginning to try to keep your life as simple as possible. Don't do too many activities, don't give yourself too many deadlines—deadlines are like big waves.

So in the beginning you should keep your life simple.

If you're learning how to drive, don't go straight to the CBD of Sydney in your first week, because it's not easy to drive there. Just drive around the quiet car parks first, when there are no cars. Then move to streets. Keep practicing. Then slowly the inner suburbs, then slowly, slowly come to the CBD.

Now when you get really, really good—that means you're able to maintain your inner stillness and calm really well—then if the tsunami of life hits you—no worries. You can take on deadlines—no problem. You can be the busiest person on the planet, with deadlines just coming at you from all directions—no problem. You'll be able to respond with peace and calm no matter what's thrown at you once you've mastered your mind.

You'll face all sorts of things in life with no problems at all—relationship difficulty, financial difficulty, bad neighbours, physical illness. No problem at all.

So, make use of a simple life, and when you're good, you can dive in the deep end.

Perseverance versus stubbornness

How do we know when to let go and when to persevere? When is perseverance just stubbornness?

In other words, when do you press the brake and when do you floor it? I'll tell you when you floor it—when you see the cops you floor it! Just joking. Don't do that.

There's a time for everything. There's a time to transplant that seedling. If it's too small when you transplant, it will be no good. There's a time for everything. We can't make a rule out of it, you see.

For example, I just said before, when you see the cops you floor it. But really, if you do that, you'll be in trouble. They'll chase you, you might have to go to court and pay a fine, or you might go to jail—it will cost you.

But what happens if you're in a bush fire and you have to drive fast to get out of there and then you see a cop? You floor it! You're not going to be worried about breaking the law. You and the cop will both be in trouble if you don't floor it! Can you see—we can't make a rule out of it.

Your heart will know. You have to learn how to follow the rules of your heart. It will know when to speak and when not to speak. It will know when to stand up and say what it feels and it will know when to keep quiet. Both outcomes will be beautiful when they come from the heart.

For example, you might be a shy person who never speaks up. But when your friends are doing something really silly and they're going to get hurt, you might raise your voice and say something, and you'll say it with so much conviction that it will stun them.

So there's a moment for everything. Your heart will know, and you can't make a rule out of it.

But having said that, I'll try to make a rule out of it! The rule is—when your heart yearns, when it's pulling you to do something, get out of the way. Let it do its thing.

Now, when there's disturbance in your mind—when you can't sleep, you can't stop thinking, you have relationship troubles, and you're thinking, "Oh, did I do something wrong?"—press 'Stop'! Stop your mind. Don't put it in neutral, because it's already rolling. Press the brake. Be strong—"I've had enough of thinking about this. I'm just going to put it aside."

Press the brake of your mind with the same oomph you would if you were driving and suddenly you saw a massive pothole on the road that would damage your car and put you in danger. How are you going to brake when that happens? It's going to be with a lot of force, isn't it? Stop your mind like that.

Well that's my rule. It's not really a rule, it's just a guide. Follow your heart—it will know what to do. But if you're not familiar with intuition, the language of the heart, then when you see the police you might do the wrong thing and floor it. And when you're caught in a bushfire, and you see the police, you might press the brake, thinking, "I don't want to get a fine." So you have to let your heart's wisdom guide you.

It is a completely different language altogether, this language of intuition. It's not black and white. It's a language of awareness, it's a sense of what feels right in that moment. Sometimes it feels like, "Should I go? Should I not? Should I go? Should I not? I'll go." And when you go, you know it's your heart pulling you there. It's not logical, but it's beautiful.

And when you follow that language, when you follow the heart, it always feels right. It fits. When you do something and you feel, "That just feels right," well, that's the language of the heart.

So you can't follow any rules. Or if there's a rule, it's 'heart rules'.

Becoming close to God

I've tried praying but I don't feel close to God. How can I feel closer to God?

Try harder.

Let's take for example getting a university education. Think of the hours of assignments and going to classes, and your determination to get the best possible marks in your exams.

If you put half the effort that you put into graduating from university—not even 100% of that, but half of that effort—towards knowing God and feeling love for God and praying for God's help, you'll be God's best friend.

It's so easy, because God is always waiting to be your best friend. All you have to do is try to be God's best friend.

So if you're praying and you still don't feel close to God—up the effort. Ask yourself—how much effort goes into graduating from a university degree? How many assignments is that? How many hours does it take to graduate?

Well, how many hours have you prayed to God for help? How many hours have you dialogued with God? How many hours have you served God in your life? Is it 1% of the hours of your university degree? Is it 2%? Is it 5%? Then bump it up to at least 50%.

God is not even asking for 100%! Just 50% of that, and you'll be God's best friend.

But we don't do that. We'd be lucky if we pray with intensity for 1% of the hours we put into getting a university degree.

When we can't figure out a university assignment and it looks like we might fail, what do we do? Better go and knock at the door of the professor—"I don't understand this assignment. Can you please help me, can you please explain?"

Well, when we have a problem in life, do we knock at God's door and ask God for help? "I'm going to fail this if you don't help me." Do we do that? No we don't. We go and do it ourself— because we think we're smart, so we try to do it on our own.

Or we pray for five seconds, ten seconds or one minute, and then think, "Oh, it doesn't work."

Did you do the same thing at university? You spent hours on your university assignments. Even if you didn't understand it, you spent hours trying to work it out. I know I did. And if I couldn't work it out, I'd speak to a friend to see if he had some good ideas. And if he couldn't help me, then I'd go to the professor.

If you make the sincere effort to be close to God and know God, just a little bit, God will get so excited. God will be running to you!

If we have no trust or belief in God, then when we're in trouble we don't ask for God's help, and when we do pray for help we pray with little faith.

So how can we feel close to God, how can we be friends with God? Friendship takes dialogue. Multiple dialogues. You don't become best friends with someone by just speaking with them for one minute, once a year. No.

In the same way, we know how to develop a friendship with God. Just a little more effort is needed. Then we'll know God.

How to serve God

How can we best serve God?

It's very easy—just *want* to. That's all that's needed.

In the same way, if you visit your parents, how best can you serve your parents? It's very simple—you want to help. That's the secret—you actually want to. You're going to say to your parents, "What can I do to help you?" And they're going to say, "OK, if you want to help, how about you start by washing the dishes and I'll think of some other things after that." But if you don't want to, you're not going to serve your parents.

So serving God is no different. God is always looking for volunteers. God has eyes that see everything—there's no distance God can't see. And even though that's the case, God can't find enough volunteers. Where are all the volunteers who want to serve God?

I remember a story from the book, *Lila Amrit*. Swami Madhavananda was spending time with Mahaprabhuji, his Master. It was challenging, but he really loved living with and serving his Master. Then somehow he got an offer for a job with the Indian government, so he said to Mahaprabhuji, "I got a job offer, I'd like to go work for the Indian government, but I want to get your blessing." And Mahaprabhuji said, "Before you go, I want to ask you one question. Who do you want to work for—the government of India or the government of saints?"

This is the question that God is asking all the time. Who do you want to be employed by—the world or God? Everybody wants to be employed by the world. So few people want to work for God. There is a shortage of volunteers.

I remember when I first arrived in Australia in 1983 and I went to Cabramatta Primary School in Sydney. I was in Mr Carney's class and sometimes he might say, "Who wants to volunteer to hand out the work sheets to everyone?" We would all sit up as tall and straight as possible, with our hand raised, thinking, "Me! Me! Choose me!" So he'd choose someone to hand out the sheets to the class.

Look at us—we had such a spirit to volunteer, to help. We felt great just when we could hand out the work sheets for the teacher.

So that's what God needs—volunteers with spirit like that. The rest is easy. The rest is natural. But if the volunteer spirit is not there, it's impossible.

Facing our negative tendencies

How can we come to really face and be honest with ourselves about our own negative tendencies?

We face our negative tendencies by knowing that's not what we want in our life. We get rid of them by sincerely wanting to get rid of them. I've never met a person who couldn't get rid of their negativity when they really wanted to. I've met people who want to dance around their negativity, and then they can't get rid of it. But I've never met a person who sincerely wanted to get rid of negativities and couldn't do it.

When we are sincere, we will face our negativity. You see, negativities come from fear, so when we face our negativities directly, that fear will just disappear, because it's not real in the first place. But until we face it, it always seems real. It's like a shadow—everywhere we go, our shadow is there. You know sometimes you're in a cemetery, and you see a shadow of a tree or something, and you think, "Is that a ghost?" You get scared. But there's no ghost, it was just a shadow.

And sometimes even your own shadow—you're walking and the shadow is moving, but because it's distorted by the trees you start to think, "Is someone following me?" But actually you stop and look and there's nobody there—it's just your own shadow!

But you've got to stop and look at it. When you stop and look at it you notice it's not real, and suddenly the fear in you disappears. There's nobody following you—"Ah, OK then." You're peaceful.

So you've got to face the negativity, and want to get rid of it. The rest—the means and the how—is a procedural thing. Once the spirit and the intention is there, you've already conquered it. Fear will vanish as if you've stepped on a rotten apple. It'll squash into nothingness.

Spiritual practice

There are so many different types of meditation and other spiritual practices. What is it that actually makes a practice a 'spiritual' practice?

A spiritual practice is anything that makes you feel more beautiful inside you.

Let me share a silly example. You know sometimes there are weight loss advertisements on TV or in a magazine and they have 'before and after' photos? They show you the person before, and then three months later, and we can see the difference.

So that's in regards to weight loss. But for spiritual practice the difference is in regards to feeling more beautiful about yourself—three months before and three months after.

So if you feel more beautiful about yourself, even if you think you haven't been doing spiritual practice, you have. And if you think you've been doing spiritual practice for the past three months, but there's no difference in the before and after, then you haven't.

So spiritual practice is anything that makes you feel more beautiful about yourself.

Don't underestimate what I'm saying about feeling more beautiful about yourself, because we're living in a world where we're trained to hate ourselves. Don't think it's an easy thing to love yourself.

So when you see results, that's when you ask, "What have I been doing?" Or sometimes it might be, "What have I not been doing?"

There are so many things that we can do to make us feel beautiful. Not what we *think* will make us feel beautiful, but what *actually* makes us feel more beautiful inside.

So spiritual practices are any activities or non-activities that lead to an increase in inner beauty and inner peace.

I find it really hard to assess my own spiritual progress. Someone might tell me I'm looking well, so perhaps I can tell that I'm growing, but on some levels it seems I haven't improved at all. How can we clearly and practically assess our own spiritual progress?

The best approach is to make sure that our practice is quality and quantity. Because if you do those two things right, inherently there'll be progress. We almost don't need to know about the progress if we do those two things right.

Because if we practise with quality but we don't do enough—there's no quantity—then progress cannot happen. And if we practise a lot and the quality is not there, then there's not much improvement either.

So therefore, our job is to make sure that we practise lots and that our practice is correct practice, efficient practice.

We should always get feedback from someone who's actually a very experienced practitioner. Preferably a Spiritual Master, because they will be able to check our progress no matter what level we're at.

And if we don't have that opportunity to double check with a Master, then we should try to look at our own progress every three months.

There are so many different criteria to use to look at our progress, but the best criterion is our equanimity of mind. That means, how long does it take for us to recover from an external or internal stimulus that causes us disturbance? How long does it take to come back to our natural state as if that never happened?

So let's say a girl breaks up with her boyfriend. How long does it take for him to get over that—where there are no more thoughts or worrying or disturbance—as if he never heard the news? How long does it take?

Or, say you get a $200 parking fine. How long does it take for you not to have that thought any more in your mind—no more disturbance? We should always try to see how long it takes. And then three months later, when we get another parking fine—how long does it take this time to not think of that anymore, to not be disturbed?

So when our equanimity of mind is stronger—when it takes less time to recover—then we know we're progressing.

And of course as we get better and better at this—when we don't even get disturbed at all, so there's no recovery needed—that's perfect mastery.

So that's the best way to check our progress. All the other ways of checking—like, 'I'm happier', or 'I love life more'—are too subjective. It's very hard to measure. We can make a mistake where we think we're progressing, but we're not.

So firstly, double check with someone that knows. And if we don't have a chance to do that, then use equanimity of mind as the criterion for measuring progress.

Overcoming fear of confrontation

How can we overcome our fear of confrontation?

Have strength. Then, because of that strength, when we confront a situation or a person, we are not afraid.

So we have to build up that strength. And strength comes from the love of oneself, the love of others, the love of the world and the love of God.

And once we have that strength in us then the fear of confrontation will not be there. The fear of anything won't be there. Because the fear of confrontation is the fear that when we have to deal with somebody we don't get along with, or encounter a difficult situation, we will get disturbed and feel uncomfortable. That's the fear.

But if we have the strength in us, then we will be comfortable in the uncomfortableness, so we can face any situation.

How to be in the present moment

What are some practical steps we can take to bring us into the present moment?

We need someone who knows the present moment to give us assurance about how to be in the present moment. Because it's possible to think you're in the present moment when you're not. And it's possible to be in the present moment and not know that. So in that sense it can be tricky.

If I've never been to India before I can't give you a tour of India. So in the same way we need someone to guide us to the present moment, and we need someone to give us confirmation so that when we're there we actually know we're there, and when we're not we actually know we're not.

When we get this feedback and then practise techniques for being present, we will be able to be in the present moment.

Start off for five seconds and know, 100%, that you're in the present moment for that whole five seconds—you'd bet your life on it. You've got to have that conviction. If you won't bet your life on it then that means you're not sure, so it's just theoretical. But the present moment is not theoretical.

So you need someone who actually knows that state, who has no doubt, and can confirm whether or not you are in the present moment. That's the most practical approach—to learn from someone who knows the present moment. Not just 'knows the present moment'—but their whole being resides permanently in the present moment.

And once we're able to be in the present moment for five seconds, and know it with conviction, then we can stretch it out to ten seconds, one minute, an hour, five hours, every moment.

Once you're able to be in the present moment every moment, at will, now it becomes very hard not to be in the present moment. But right now, for most of us, it's the other way round.

So the short answer is, we need someone that knows the present moment to guide us, give us assurance, and the rest is just practise, practise, practise. That's all.

Overcoming self-importance

How can I overcome my strong sense of self-importance?

We have to re-wire our mind—see things from a different angle, see things from a different light. Because we've been seeing things from the light that to be *something* is beneficial, and to be *nothing* is not beneficial.

All our life we've been trained to be something. To be a football star, to be a famous singer, to be a model, to be the CEO of a company. We've been trained that to be something is beneficial. So because of that, we see this sense of importance as beneficial, and we will not do anything to the contrary of that.

Let me demonstrate with an example. Let's say I go to the monthly Byron Bay market and I make an announcement saying, "Anybody who wants to learn how to be nothing, come to me. I'll teach you. I'll show you how to master it faster than you can imagine. I'm a Master at it. I'll give you free food and board!" People are not going to come because no-one understands the benefit of being nothing. As a matter of fact, they might think I'm mad and call the market security for saying weird things like that!

But if I make an announcement saying, "I can make you famous, I can make you rich, I can help you win Grammy awards!"—people will be following me everywhere I go!

The benefit of being totally nothing is that you cannot be hurt. Only something can be hurt. Nothing cannot be hurt.

For example, the air—the air is like nothing. Try to punch the air—is the air going to be hurt? No. Swear at the air. Is it offended? Say to the air, "You're smelly." Does it get upset? No. But if you say to somebody, "You've got bad breath," that person's going to be hurt.

My Master Amma used to say that in a tornado big trees will be uprooted, but the grass never gets uprooted. In other words, being low, being nothing, is beneficial.

If someone screams at you and you know you're nothing, would you have any reaction or be defensive? You're nothing, so it just passes by you.

It's the sense of self-importance that is the formula for feeling miserable, the formula for being hurt, the formula for being angry, the formula for feeling insecure. And it is the formula for feeling superior and putting people down, the formula for hurting other people's feelings. Nothing will never hurt someone's feelings— how could it? Nothing can't hurt. Only something can hurt something—nothing can't hurt something.

So we have to re-wire ourself, shift our understanding of what is beneficial—what enhances our life and what destroys our life. We have to understand that. And once we understand that, then we start to train ourself with the intention, passion and determination to be humble like a blade of grass. To be nothing.

Then that self-importance will just disappear like a bank robber when the police car comes—very quickly! As soon as they hear the siren, they're gone. The false sense of importance will be gone like that.

The benefit of a Guru

Why is it beneficial to have a Guru?

They have experience. They've already walked the path to enlightenment. Quite often they've done it in many, many lifetimes.

Let's take for example trying to get a licence to drive a car. Imagine you are a very nervous driver, so you know you can bomb out in the driving test. You just know that, so you start to look for a driving instructor.

Now, do you want a driving instructor that has no experience, has never driven before, and borrowed his brother's licence to put on the dashboard? Or do you want a professional driver with 20 years of driver training experience? If the price was the same, which one would you use?

You'd use someone who has more experience—they've done it before. They know how to read traffic, they know how to handle dangerous right turns, they know how to change lanes, they know all the blind spots, they know what to do when a big truck is in the lane right next to you, they know the safest moves, they don't panic.

So in the same way, it's good to have a Guru, because they have experience. They know all the traffic jams of the mind, they know all the red lights, they know all the potholes on the road where you can skid off and have an accident, they know those bends in the road where the signage says 80 km/hr but it should really be 40 km/hr. They tell you all these things. They have experience, they know the mind inside out.

They help you learn how to drive through the traffic of this world, so you can be relaxed and use this vehicle called the body and the mind to weave through the traffic like an experienced taxi driver in the Sydney CBD. They're very relaxed, cruising through all the tricky streets and traffic jams. So a true Guru makes it easier to reach the goal.

Part 3

Deeper Reflections

"To love everyone—that's the goal. Because if you love everyone, you're going to be happy, and you're going to have perfect mind control."

The purpose of life

In a nutshell, what is the purpose of human life?

First, I'll tell you what is *not* the purpose of human life. That is, to come to this planet and just think that we're here to complete a set of tasks and then die. To have a long 'to-do' list, and when you do one thing you tick it off—go to school, own a car, get married, have children, buy a house. Tick if off—do this thing, do that thing, fix the fence, pick the kids up from school, cook the dinner. Do all these types of things, and then die.

That's not the purpose of life.

We came to this planet to experience the beauty of our divine Self—to actually experience the magnificence of this divine Self in the human body, amidst all these tasks.

The tasks are not the goal, the tasks are just the backdrop. The goal is the dance. You're dancing in front of the backdrop of these activities.

You're here to experience the divine dance. You're here to celebrate your divine Self. You're here to experience your seed of greatness. You're here to see this seed become an oak tree. You're here to flower. You're here to experience beauty, in unimaginable ways. That's the purpose of life.

What you're talking about sounds really wonderful, but do many people actually fulfil that purpose in their life?

There have been thousands that have fulfilled their purpose. The ones that wish for it will have it fulfilled. The ones who don't have that wish won't have it fulfilled. The issue is not that many people can't fulfil their purpose in life, but that they actually don't want to.

God is always waiting to bless people. God is always waiting to turn on the music so you can do this dance. But there are no dancers. Nobody's dressed up for the bush dance or the salsa dance. So God says, "Oh, I'll put my music away."

But yes, there have been thousands of people who danced this dance. Amidst the chaos of life, they're just in absolute calmness and stillness and peacefulness. Amidst the pull from all different directions, amidst the heaviness of life, they're absolutely light and joyful.

So there are many people.

Why think, "Have there been many people? I don't see many." Why not think, "There *have* been people who have achieved that, who lived like that, so why not me too?" Why not?

Must we do something only because millions do it first? Or do we need only one person to show us that it's possible to live that way, and then we strive towards that?

For example, if you are in a city, say Mumbai in India, and you're really hungry and you want to know where they sell some delicious curries, how many people do you ask? Do you have to ask a million people, "Where's the nearest delicious curry shop?" You don't, do you? You only have to ask one person. You don't wait for a million people to tell you about a curry shop, and approve that curry shop.

So in the same way, all you need to know is that at least one person on this planet has lived like that—danced this song of love on the backdrop of activities and busyness. All you need is to know of one.

But there happens to be more than one anyway! Thousands. And even though those thousands are a very minute fraction of the billions on the planet, all you need is one.

When I was a spiritual seeker, I always felt that if one person has attained enlightenment, I can do it too. Why not?

What have they done? I'll do the same. How do they think? I'll think the same. Who do they love? I'll love the same. Who do they pray to? I'll pray to the same. What do they eat? I'll eat the same. How do they walk? I'll walk the same. What spiritual practices did they do? I'll do the same. Why not?

I always felt like that. So I knew that if I don't achieve it, it's not because it's not possible—if I don't achieve it it's because I don't want it enough.

Being present

In the West now it's quite common to hear people talking about living in the here and now, and being 'present'. But what does being present really look like?

It means you're not in your head space. It means you're here. You're here, and you know it.

If I ask you, "Are you in this room right now?" do you doubt that you're in this room? Or are you 100% clear that you are? If your answer is yes, then you *are* right here right now. You're here in this room, and you're not somewhere else. You know that. You're here in this room right now. That's called the here and now.

To know that—everywhere you are, whatever you're doing, every moment—that's called being in the here and now.

The here and now doesn't change, it's just the context—the backdrop—that is changing. But the here and now is exactly the same.

Hypothetically, you could be on a field running on the grass, in this moment. Then it will feel to you that you're in the here and now on the field. But if you're running on the field and you're in your head, thinking about the future, thinking about the past, thinking about all sorts of things, then you're on the field, but you're not there. Physically you're there, but in spirit you're somewhere else—your awareness is somewhere else. You're in the box of your mind, in your thoughts.

So what does being present look like? It's got a million faces. It depends on where you are, who you're with, etc. If you're swimming in the ocean, the here and now will be that you're there in the water, in the ocean, in that moment, and you're fully aware of it.

The present moment has a million faces.

How can I actually let go of the thinking and the planning and the organising, so that I can be in the here and now, and just have the faith that all that needs to happen will somehow happen?

You need to retrain yourself in order to get out of the habit of thinking and into the habit of letting go and surrendering to the moment.

In the same way, when you've been walking forward most of your life, and suddenly you have to walk backwards everywhere you go, you need a lot of practice to learn to do that properly.

So it just takes retraining. We have picked up the habit of thinking a lot, so all we have to do is pick up a new habit of *not* thinking a lot. That's all.

Recognising an enlightened Master

Can you give some advice on how someone can recognise whether a person is an enlightened Master?

Well, the first thing is—only an enlightened person can really recognise an enlightened person. However, there are many cues, many pointers, that can help us recognise one.

A typical cue is an enlightened person has perfect equanimity of mind. That means nothing disturbs them. There's no 'up' and there's no 'down'.

With these eyes you can't tell, because it sometimes looks like an enlightened person is excited and at other times they're not speaking much. But these eyes are not accurate, because inside the person there is perfect equanimity.

If the enlightened person is laughing aloud, there's a lot of activity, a lot of noise. And if suddenly they're in a quiet mood, they're laughing too, but you just can't hear the laugh! They're laughing inside, but from the outside it looks very different.

So they have this perfect equanimity of mind—there's no bad mood for even one second. It's just not possible, because they know who they are.

Another quality is that they have perfect surrender. There's no resistance in their life. Their life is like a leaf falling—whichever way the wind blows, they just go with that.

The enlightened person won't have any resistance if somebody hates them or if somebody loves them—it doesn't affect them inside. Whether someone praises them or speaks nasty words to them, it doesn't affect them.

So they have this perfect surrender to life.

And because they have that surrender, because they have no resistance, they are very light, so they laugh a lot. They may not laugh out loud, but there's great joy in them. Some might laugh more outwardly and some might laugh more inwardly, but there's great joy in them.

Another way to recognise an enlightened Master is they love life. They love everybody—people who like them and people who hate them. In their heart they love everyone.

Sometimes on the outside they can do actions that look like they're not loving, but it's always sponsored by love inside. Always. We just don't know that, that's all. They might scream at a person, but that scream is just full of love, sponsored by love.

If you ever want to be screamed at by somebody, make sure it's an enlightened person. It'll do you so much good—because it's sponsored by love, you see. It's much, much better to be screamed at by an enlightened person than to be praised by someone who doesn't love you.

Another typical sign is that they are full of wisdom.

And the true Master is always there, guiding others, protecting others. They never give up. Disciples give up, but the Master never gives up.

So these are a few ways to recognise an enlightened Master.

Body, mind, spirit

What is the mind-body-spirit connection?

We were designed by God as a triune being—that means we are three-in-one. As a human being, we are body, mind, spirit.

The body is the most dense—it's solid. So you can clap your hands and it makes a noise, whereas you can't make a sound like that with the soul.

The mind is really a bundle of thoughts, a forest of thoughts. Thoughts are less dense than the body, but more dense than the soul.

And the soul is least dense.

We understand density from science—solid, liquid, gas. Gas is the least dense. It's the same with our triune nature—body, mind, spirit. The most real part of us is the spirit—it's the lightest part of us.

So the path towards enlightenment is the path towards being the lightest you can be. And this can only happen by shifting your vibration more towards the spirit or soul part of the triune being. Then you become more soul-like.

Now, when something is more dense, it's less flexible, right? A rock is less flexible than water. Water can go into a tiny crack, but you can't push a big rock into a tiny crack—it's less flexible.

So when our vibration shifts towards being more dense, more 'I am the body'-focussed, then we become less flexible and less adaptable to the world around us. When someone is rude to us, we can't adjust to it. So we become less flexible, or more rigid. Even when we walk, we walk more rigidly. And we talk more rigidly. Basically, we feel less happy, and have more problems.

The next dense level is the mind. The vibration at this level is less dense than the body but is still very dense in comparison to the soul. So if we reside more in the mind, we will feel more heavy and have more suffering. But if we try to switch off our mind—our thoughts—and we identify less with that level, we will become more soul-like.

Problems are always at the dense levels of the body and the mind. At the soul level, there are no problems. The soul doesn't have any problems. So we need to try to shift away from the body vibration, bypass the forest of the mind, and reside more and more in the soul.

When we dis-identify from the body and the mind, that immediately puts us into soul-consciousness, or light vibration. For example, when we are more kind and more loving, that's more soul-like, so we become more light, and feel more happy.

Understanding how the body-mind-spirit connection works means we can apply this knowledge in our everyday life, so that we are able to live a more happy, peaceful and enlightened life.

Enlightenment

What is enlightenment?

Enlightenment is when you have no more suffering. You have no emotional trauma and you are not trapped in your emotion. You go through life fearlessly, no matter what you face.

One Master was asked, "Do you have any preference in life?" And he said, "No." And they said to him, "But if you had one preference in life, what would it be?" He said, "If I had one preference in life, it would be that whatever shows up is my preference."

So enlightenment is like that—whatever shows up is your preference. Wherever and however life takes you, you totally embrace it. You're grateful for it. The so-called good and bad, you're grateful for both, equally.

Another way to look at it is that you are totally surrendered to life, like a leaf that falls off a tree—the destiny of that leaf could go in any direction, depending on which way the wind blows in that moment. The leaf has no resistance. It doesn't have any preference to go in the opposite direction to the wind.

So enlightenment is a totally surrendered state where God runs your life.

Is enlightenment something that we should be striving for?

If we want to be peaceful and happy, and go through life equipped to enjoy it, then we need to strive towards enlightenment. If we don't care about being happy and peaceful and fearless and joyful in life, then we should not search for enlightenment.

So it's all up to us. There's no 'should' and 'should not'. It's all about what outcome we want in our life.

Do enlightened people really have supernatural powers?

Some do and some don't. It is not supernatural power that makes a person enlightened.

There are people who have no supernatural power who are enlightened. And there are people with supernatural power who are not enlightened. In other words, they are people who have supernatural power but still have emotional suffering.

So they're two different things. It's like comparing Vietnamese and German—they're two different languages that have nothing in common. It just happens to be that some German people can speak Vietnamese, and some Vietnamese people can speak German. But those two languages actually have nothing in common.

Of course, naturally, when we witness a person with supernatural power, we think, "Wow, I can't do that, so they must be something special."

But don't see things with these eyes. When you close your eyes, in your heart you can perceive whether a person is an enlightened person. If your heart is tuned in, you can perceive an enlightened person.

So supernatural power and enlightenment are totally un-related—they are two different things. It is not supernatural power that makes someone an enlightened person, but their qualities of perfect equanimity, perfect selflessness and unconditional love.

Meditation practice

Can a person progress spiritually if they don't meditate?

Yes. There's not one person on this planet that is not progressing spiritually. Just to be alive, you're progressing. Now the bit that can vary is—how fast do you want to grow?

And how fast has nothing to do with comparison or com-petition. It's not a sport. In the history of this planet, spirituality has never been a sport where there's competition. It's just a solo, individual wish to grow at a certain rate and remember who we are, our true Self.

Now, if our wish is to grow fast, then meditation is a must, because our true Self is meditation. Not a meditation technique, but the meditation state. Meditation techniques are tools to help bring us to the meditation state—the present moment.

So if we want to grow fast, then we have to know how to be in that meditation state. When we say 'grow fast', what does that mean? We know what it looks like when a seedling grows into a big tree, but when we talk about spiritual growth, what are we growing towards?

Well, we tend to identify ourself as the body and the mind, which is very limited. It's very boxed up—it's like living in a mansion but you only hang around the bathroom and never use the whole house. But if you 'grow' spiritually, your knowledge of yourself expands. You become more open and loving, and start to use more of your potential.

The highest expansiveness is called the meditation state or the supreme state. And if we're not trying to be in that state, how are we going to grow from the limited body and mind? So the meditation state is critical for spiritual growth.

Now, meditation techniques are tools to help bring you to the meditation state, but even if you're using these tools, there's no guarantee they are going to bring you to the meditation state. On the other hand, there are people who use no meditation techniques at all, and they just go directly to the meditation state.

It is not just sitting down and closing your eyes that you can call meditation. Prayer, mantras, and other spiritual techniques are all ultimately to help bring you to the meditation state, or your true Self.

Selfless service is another very powerful method to bring you to the meditation state. Because if you're kind to someone, it's going to make you feel beautiful about yourself, and when you feel beautiful about yourself your mind will stop. That chattering that speaks garbage all the time will stop. And because your mind stops, you'll feel peaceful, and when you feel peacefulness you're in the meditation state.

So it's critical to strive to be in the meditation state. Every meditator out there should be asking, "Am I in the meditation state when I am meditating?" And, "If I meditate for half an hour, how much of that half an hour am I actually in that meditation state?" You should know that, if you want to progress spiritually.

Sometimes when I'm chanting my Guru mantra, I find it very difficult and I start to wonder if I should do a different meditation practice. But is that just the mind trying to defeat that meditation?

See, the mind does its thing, which is—create division. That's its job description.

When you use mantra meditation, that brings you to the present moment, which is 'oneness'. Now, because the mind always does its thing, which is to divide, it separates you from the universe, from the oneness. The mind will always bring you to that separation in the form of thoughts. It will always do that.

So when we first start mantra practice, the mind will do that to us. But when we become better at the practice, more skilful at it, then we become very sharp, and more aware. Then, our concentration will bring us to the present moment, and when the mind takes us away from our concentration we will know straight away. We will know, "Ah, that feels different." It's like you're sitting on a hot day and there's no breeze at all, it's absolutely still, and suddenly you feel a cool breeze on your face. You will notice the difference.

So during meditation, your mind will take you away from your concentration. It will happen. And you should expect that to happen, in the same way that an Australian cricketer playing against the Poms in the Ashes should expect them to try to get him out. You should have that expectation, and that way you become more prepared. There's more focus in your meditation practice so that you will be able to defeat the opposition—in this case it's not the English cricketers, it's your own mind.

So expect the mind to distract you. That's its job.

Awareness

What is awareness and why is it so important to be aware of our thoughts?

Awareness is the bridge between theory and practice.

My Master shares a story to illustrate this. There was a wealthy businessman who believed that whatever a person is thinking about at the time of their death will determine what they become in their next life. So he named his three sons after the gods Krishna, Rama and Shiva. He thought that at the moment of death he's sure to call one of his sons to come and be near him, so he named his sons after gods.

The moment of his death came, and he called out to his sons, "Krishna! Rama! Shiva!" All three came as fast as they could to be with their father. But suddenly the businessman said, "My boys, if you're all here, who's running the business?"

So he had called out God's name, but his whole life was so focussed on money that his last thought was about who was going to run his business! He didn't think of God at the moment of his death, because the awareness wasn't there. The strategy was there, the theory was there, but the awareness wasn't there.

So the purpose of spiritual training is to increase this awareness. When that awareness increases to a certain level, then there will be a bridge between theory and practice. Otherwise you can do courses and retreats and study all the spiritual knowledge, but in the moment where it counts you won't remember it. Like the businessman.

So what we need is few theories but great awareness, then we can actually apply and live all the spiritual principles that lead to happiness and peace of mind.

Thoughts

Sometimes it seems that thinking is actually more fun than not thinking. Not thinking can feel like nothing. So why should we practise to not think?

Inherently, there's nothing wrong with thinking. It's like a Formula One vehicle—it just happens to go incredibly fast and you can lose control very easily. Similarly, there's nothing wrong with thinking at all—until you have a spin-out and end up in a mental hospital.

Thought can be fun. Imagination and creativity are from the mind. For example, cooking delicious meals can come from using your mind creatively. That marination of thoughts can be fun.

The mind is magnificent. It can build the Opera House, design the Harbour Bridge. There are many beautiful things you can do with it. But if you can't control it, if you can't switch it off at will, there's a problem.

You see, we should only be thinking for between 1% and 5% of our day. That's all we need to think to experience the fun of it.

But where it creates destruction in our life is when we keep on pressing the 'repeat' button.

You know sometimes when you watch a video clip online it just replays immediately after if finishes. In the same way, we think about things, then keep on replaying them like that. If we replay something one time or two times, that's fair enough. But 50 times!

And maybe you don't mind 50 replays, but here is where the problem lies—every time you think, it dissipates energy. It's like if you have a gas bottle for your BBQ, every time you light it, it uses gas. So when you think, this uses the gas of your vitality.

And if you keep it running every day, that bottle's going to get low pretty quickly. And when that bottle is flat, they'll diagnose you with depression. You haven't got energy. You feel flat. That's just psychologically, but of course when you feel flat your immune system goes down also. And when you feel flat your awareness is very low, so you can't discriminate between healthy food and nourishing food. So you eat junk food and it makes you more flat. You go on the course of self-destruction.

So if your goal is self-destruction, then continuous thinking and not learning the ability to stop thinking is the way to go. If you think it's fun when you've got no vitality and your immune system is weak and you get all sorts of physical diseases and mental illness—if you think that's fun, then that's fun!

But before we think what's fun or not, we should know the full story, not half the story. Where it's problematic is everybody's doing it—thinking. We're taught, 'Think and grow rich'. We're taught, 'Think your way to success'. We're taught, 'Think carefully about what you're doing'. And if you're being a bit silly in the classroom, the teacher will say, "Stop that. Think about how you're behaving."

So everybody's thinking. We're trained to think that it's good to think. But that is not the full story. The truth is this planet is plagued with mental illness and it's caused by excessive thinking—so we should ask ourself, is that really fun?

How can I become a witness to my thoughts rather than being caught up in them?

Firstly, you have to understand that there is such a thing as thoughts—that the existence of thoughts is real, it's not just some concept or idea.

And then, to be a witness to your thoughts, you have to be able to see your thoughts. In other words, you want to be aware of whatever thought goes through your mind.

Imagine you're a blind person and you're going for a job as a security guard for the Sydney Harbour Bridge. The job is to just pace back and forth along the bridge in case someone tries to damage it.

Now, if a person was blind, would they get the security guard job? No—because a condition of the job is that they have to be able to see.

So we have to be able to see our thoughts, and to be able to see our thoughts we need a set of special eyes. Our physical eyes can't see thoughts because they are designed to see what is physical, but a different set of eyes can see the invisible. These are the eyes of awareness. Without these eyes of awareness, witnessing thoughts is just a theory.

So witnessing our thoughts sounds great, but the question is—has our level of awareness reached a certain point where we're able to see our thoughts with 20-20 vision? Then we can witness. Then the security guard can say, "I've done my whole shift and there was nothing suspicious whatsoever. I did not witness anybody doing the wrong thing."

So we have to basically practise how to increase our awareness—through one-pointed meditation, through prayer, through being in the presence of an enlightened Master, through remaining open-hearted, through serving the world, through surrendering all our negativities, and trusting that God does everything for the best.

We have to practise this for our awareness to increase enough to be able to witness our thoughts rather than just being caught up in them.

Dwelling in the present moment

How do we progress from bringing ourself to the present moment, to staying in the present moment for a long time?

A person might know how to pedal a bicycle for, say, ten rounds of pedalling, without falling off. Now imagine asking that person, "How do you stay pedalling for longer? How do you pedal for two hours?" What's the person going to say?

They will say, "Well, when I first started, I couldn't pedal for ten rounds because I would fall off. But now I'm able to pedal for ten rounds without falling off, then after that I just keep on pedalling."

So to be in the present moment for longer—whether it's through mindfulness or any other practice—you have to be able to stay in the present moment and not 'fall off'. You have to be able to be in the present moment for at least ten seconds.

After you're able to do it for ten seconds without falling off, then continue practising diligently to stay in the present moment as long as possible and as frequently as possible each day.

The only way a person can't pedal for more than ten rounds is if they stop—because they don't want to or it's not fun anymore or they don't have an interest in it, etc.

But if a person has an interest in it, and they're able to be present and know it with 100% clarity—not just theoretically—then if they can do it for ten seconds they can do it as long as they like.

So it's just practice, that's all. It may not be as easy as pedalling a bike, but it's the same truth, the same principle.

Advice for spiritual practice

Are there any words of advice that you can share for someone who's an absolute beginner at spiritual practice?

Some sage, I think in China, said, "The journey of a thousand miles begins with one step." And I know Sir Donald Bradman was not a legendary cricket player the first time he walked onto the pitch. Be clear about that.

So, there's hope for all of us!

It doesn't matter where you're at, it's where you're going that counts. You could be the worst at something, in any field, but if you keep on taking one step at a time, one step at a time, you could be an expert at it in no time. You'll be amazed.

So just take the steps. Keep on practising.

It's like—not that long ago I was walking up Mount Warning and it seemed to take forever. There were so many steps, you just never got to the top. But I knew if my legs kept on moving, I would get there.

Occasionally when someone was on their way back down I'd ask, "How far is it to go?" They might say, "Oh, probably half an hour." So then I'd go back to one step at a time, one step at a time. You'd be amazed—suddenly you see, "Oh, I'm nearly there." As long as you keep walking.

That's it. There's no secret.

And what makes us walk? Because we want to get there. We want to get to the top of Mount Warning to see the panoramic view. We want to have—not a bird's eye view, but God's eye view. We want to be on top of the world and see what the world looks like.

Are there some words you can share with someone who's been doing spiritual practices for many, many years?

Two things. Keep on practising and keep on checking your progress. You don't want to be somebody who's practising for 20 years and the 'before and after' shot is the same. You don't want to do that.

You should always check.

In our life, we do this kind of checking all the time. When I used to drive from Sydney to Melbourne it often seemed like I'd never get there, and I was always checking the kilometres.

Every 20, 30, 50 kilometres there's a sign by the road that says how many kilometres left to Melbourne. So I'd think, "Oh, I'm getting closer." But I always checked.

So make sure you're moving forward.

You should practise and check. Make sure that you feel more calm and peaceful. Make sure that when someone is rude to you, you're more relaxed and calm about it—you're improving. Make sure that when life doesn't go your way, like relationship or health problems, you don't feel down all the time.

Make sure you're improving. Practise and check. Before you know it, you'll collide with freedom.

Sometimes it can feel difficult to continue with spiritual practices because I get to a point where they feel boring or difficult. Where can I find the motivation to continue if I'm just feeling lazy or uninterested?

If we feel lazy or uninterested that simply means we must not truly understand the benefits of something for ourself, for our life.

For example, imagine you haven't got much money and you hear that the kebab shop in town is having a promotion tomorrow where you can get a free kebab and a hundred dollars. I want to ask a question—how do you motivate yourself to go get that free kebab and a hundred dollars? Do you need me to inspire you? No. Do you need to read inspirational books? No. Why? Because you understand the benefit of it.

So when we think about spiritual practice and we're bored and we feel it's weird or it doesn't work or whatever, that means we don't understand the benefit of it—how it enhances our life.

For me, when I looked at the difference in myself after doing spiritual practice, I saw that I was feeling more beautiful, and it made me curious—"Wow, how beautiful can I feel? What's the limit? I'm curious."

So no-one needed to tell me to do spiritual practice, because I understood the benefit.

When I first learnt meditation, in my first year of university, I'd meditate for an hour in the morning and an hour at night, sitting on the carpet. I didn't even understand that you're allowed to meditate on a cushion—I had no idea! My bottom would get sore towards the end of the hour and I'd think, "I wonder how these people are meditating and their bottoms are not sore. What's wrong with me?"

But I was feeling more peaceful, more beautiful.

My father used to go to my room and open my door, and have a look to see what I was doing in there. He never said, "Keep it up, son." I've never had anybody who personally encouraged me to do this. But I had many people who discouraged me!

So why did I continue? Because I understood, "Wow, it benefits me. I feel beautiful. I don't want to walk around feeling flat and drained." Nobody needed to teach me what being flat and drained felt like—I experienced plenty of that, so I knew the difference.

So if we're bored and feel this is difficult, that means we must do more contemplation. We must ask ourself in a much deeper way, "Why am I doing this spiritual practice? For what reason?" We have to ask ourself a lot more deeply.

Are we doing a meditation retreat or joining a group to do spiritual practice so we can encourage each other to practise more? Or are we there to look for a partner? There could be all sorts of reasons. Are we just lonely at home and we want to speak to someone so we don't feel weird at home by ourself all the time?

I'm not saying there's anything wrong with those reasons, but if we have those reasons as our motivation, when we get home we will find it very boring to meditate!

So if we feel bored, we should contemplate and ask ourself, "Why am I doing this? Is this doing me any good? Why am I doing this?"

And if we ask why, if we investigate, and we realise that the benefits of spiritual practice are what we wish for in our life, then we're unstoppable.

On your journey did you find that spiritual practices became easier as you got closer to the goal of self-realisation?

Yes. Like when you first play tennis, you hit a backhand and the ball is just flying over the fence or hitting the net! But after three months, you can hit a lot better.

So as you go forward it gets easier and easier.

When a baby first starts to take steps after the crawling stage, within days they get better and better. So in the same way, I found I got better and better at this. It seemed more easy, more natural.

When I was a seeker, the first thing I did when I woke up in the morning—doesn't matter what time it was, work or no work—before I brushed my teeth, before I went to the toilet or did anything, I'd sit up and get my blanket and wrap it over me, and I would meditate. First thing.

I looked forward to that, because I knew that when I got to work it was going to feel heavy. I didn't look forward to that!

So for that time, I'd just sit down and relax and feel my heart, feel peaceful, just enjoy my inner tranquility. Then I'd go to work. Even though I didn't like the work, it was a bit better after meditating.

Without a doubt, over time it gets easier and easier, as you get results.

Selflessness

Is doing selfless service a way to help erase our conditioning?

That is one of the ways to purify your conditioning—and perhaps the best way.

Why is it the best way? Because the best way is the easiest way.

To sit in one place and just try to remember the love in your heart—to directly feel your true Self, the source within you—that's not easy. But to do a selfless act is very easy.

For example, if you have two mangoes and you're eating by yourself and then another person looks like they'd like to have one—it is not hard to give one to that person. Anyone can do that.

So in that sense, selflessness is the best way, because that's the easiest way to erase conditioning.

Love for all

If there was just one thing for a spiritual seeker to focus on, what would you say that should be?

To love everyone—that's the goal. Because if you love everyone, you're going to be happy, and you're going to have perfect mind control.

Strive to love everyone. It may not be easy, but try your best. That's the best practice you can do.

We can all do that.

Does love for the Guru or love for God achieve the same outcome?

Yes it does.

In the beginning, the love of the Guru will feel like you're loving a person—your beloved. But the more your love grows and the more there's a heartfelt love and connection with the Guru, then automatically there's a love for everybody in the world.

What the Guru may not tell you is that, "I represent everyone. I actually don't exist. So when you love me, you are loving everyone." Because the Guru or God *is* everyone—that is the nature of a Guru or the nature of God. So if you love a Guru beautifully, sincerely, innocently, like a child loves their mother, then naturally you'll love everyone. Actually, you cannot *not* love everyone, even if you try. It just happens naturally.

So to love the Guru is a great way to love everyone. It's a way of training to love everyone, because from the perspective of your mind, you see the Guru as just one person. So you're only loving one person and you don't have to try to love the seven billion other people on the planet. Imagine you're training to love seven billion people—where do you start? But to love one person—that's doable.

Is it necessary to be in the physical presence of the Guru to tune into them or to really cultivate that love for them?

There's no rule that says we can't tune into a Guru's heart, or love any person, if we're not in their physical proximity. There's no rule that says that—we know that from our life experience.

Sometimes a mother is living far away from her children. They could be refugees and their family is split up, with the children going overseas first and the mother still in their native land. So the distance is far, physically, but the love is near.

Now, having said that, if you were separated from your mother when you were a baby and haven't seen her since, it's more difficult to feel love for her. It's possible, but it's a lot harder.

There's no rule that says to love someone you need to be physically close, but it is much easier.

So that physical presence with a Master—when you're seeing them every day, you're meeting them, you're interacting with them—can create a closeness, a special bond. And that helps you to develop trust and love of the Master.

Then when you go far away, that bond is still there—the feeling of closeness is still there. You're still connected. Even though you could be thousands of miles away, that feeling is there.

Anybody who lives with a Spiritual Master, who spends a lot of time with a Spiritual Master, who has a connection with a Spiritual Master—when they go away, they will know what I'm talking about.

But that's no different to the example I said with the mother and child. The mother and daughter have a bond from birth, which is developed in that physical closeness—the baby is in the mother's womb for nine months, the mother breastfeeds her baby—that bond is developed in that physical closeness.

So when the family is split up as refugees, the child lives overseas, but the love, the bond, is close—in their love they are as close as if the baby is still in the mother's womb.

So, you don't need physical closeness to love the Master, or to love anybody. But being in the presence helps—physical closeness helps to begin with.

Having said that, there are people who have no physical closeness with the Master and yet they feel deeply connected to the Master. St Francis of Assisi is one of them. He never spent physical time with Jesus because he was born hundreds of years after Jesus was on planet Earth, but that didn't affect the love and closeness in his heart towards Jesus. Their connection was both distance-less and timeless.

Oneness

What does the term 'oneness' refer to?

It means one and not two. There's only one of us—there's no 'us' and 'them'. Oneness is knowing that, understanding that, and living that.

What appears to be two is actually one. There's one of me, but the me in me is everywhere. Everywhere, I see me. There's no you and me, it's just me.

If you said that to someone they would probably think you're egotistic—"It's just me!" But it's true. There's just one of us. That's oneness.

When you live that way, how are you going to hate another? There's no 'other'. That person that you call another is you. So how do you hate another?

Are you going to go and attack another? That's me attacking me. Somehow you just won't do that, you see.

Are you going to be afraid of another? That means me afraid of me.

So there's only one and not two.

On the outside, with these eyes, all you see is two, three, four, five, etc. But what these eyes see is inaccurate. If you live according to these eyes, you'll be in trouble. Let's take the perspective of a racist person. It is what they see with their eyes that allows them to be racist. If they have no eyes, if they can't see the person's nationality, how can they be racist against them? They can't.

So when you use these physical eyes, you won't see the truth. All you see is an illusion that you are separate from others.

If everyone lived the truth that there's only one of us, there would be no need for border patrol, there'd be no need for passports, there'd be no need for security guards, there'd be no need to lock up your house.

So oneness means knowing that there's only one of us, and expressing that in your everyday life.

Every time you don't like a person, know that you're seeing things as two. "That person's rude to me, I don't like that person,"—you're seeing things as 'me' versus 'them'. In that moment, remember the truth—there's only one of us.

And when you live according to that, you won't be afraid. You'll love everyone, because everyone is you.

Seeing divinity in others

How can we come to see the divinity in others rather than focussing on their shortcomings?

Well it's not easy! See we're living in a world based on the philosophy of 'buyer beware'. I learned that in legal studies—in Latin it's *caveat emptor*—buyer beware. Which basically means don't trust anybody. We're living in a world like this.

Within that framework of 'don't trust anybody', now try to see divinity in everybody. There's a bit of a clash there!

So how are we going to do that? How are we going to be able to see divinity in everybody and everything? How are we going to see everything and everybody as perfect creations of the Divine?

Well for you to be able to see the divinity in everybody you have to throw out that mindset of 'don't trust anybody'. I'm not saying don't take care, but I'm talking about the attitude of not trusting anybody. That has to go out the window. We have to be able to live life feeling that if somebody tricks us, "I'm open to that. It's just another experience in my life."

For example, let's say you're really wealthy and you enter a relationship with someone who is financially poor. Then after three years of marriage there's a divorce and they take 70% of your wealth. Well, if you throw out the caveat emptor attitude, you won't let that experience shape the next relationship. You'll use your intuition in trusting the next person you meet and once you trust, it's total trust. You're not afraid. You're not afraid to lose anything, you're not afraid to be tricked by anybody, you're not afraid to be looked down upon by anybody. Your life is not damage-control.

So it's not easy. It takes a lot of throwing out of the old. A massive clean-up is needed to get rid of all those fear-based beliefs.

Surrender

What is the benefit of surrender?

The benefit of surrender is that you feel light, immediately.

When you're trying to build a house made of stone and you're carrying 50 kilos of stones on your back to the building site, now, when you finally drop the 50 kilos, how does it feel? It feels very light. It feels like, "Oh, thank God I surrendered that. This just feels so much better."

In the same way, when we surrender our false identity, when we surrender the stones of our mind, then suddenly we feel like, "Thank God. Ooh, I feel so light. It feels so light."

Then you can jump, then you can bounce, then you can skip, then you can dance. Because you feel very light.

But with that burden of 50 kilos, don't even think about jumping, don't think about skipping, don't think about dancing.

How can we surrender to what actually 'is' rather than wanting to change the way things are?

Surrendering to 'what is' happens after a person has spent so much time trying to create an ideal life—change things, change other people, change the outside circumstances—that they get worn out and realise that it doesn't work. So they give up trying to change the outside, and simply surrender to life.

If you're trying to live an ideal life, you're going to struggle, because an ideal life doesn't exist. It is a life that your mind has manufactured and interpreted from all the data that you picked up along the way in your life.

'The ideal partner'. What silliness. Try to look for an ideal partner. In every relationship there are problems! There's no such thing as an ideal partner. There's an ideal attitude, but not an ideal partner.

There's no such thing as an ideal family. Sometimes people born in a poor family think, "Oh, that's not ideal." And people born in a rich family feel that's not ideal either! So what is an ideal family?

You see, we naturally stop trying to seek and pursue these ideals outside of us when we've tried it so much that we're out of steam.

When you're out of steam, you realise deep down that it hasn't worked, that your life has become an absolute mess. You're not telling this to other people—you might appear confident, you might be professional, you might have university qualifications. But deep inside you know your life is an absolute mess.

When you have experimented in that way, and it has not produced fruit, something happens to make you question things. You can call it God's grace, you can call it true intelligence, you can call it luck—whatever—but you start to kind of question. "Something's wrong. Something's wrong."

Then suddenly something inside you will make you stop looking for solutions on the outside—chasing the ideals. You drop all ideals.

Now when you drop everything like that, are you going to be thinking much about life? No. Because a lot of thinking happens when you're continually adjusting, fixing, trying to find what's ideal—ideal partner, ideal this, ideal that. It breeds a lot of thinking and strategising. And when all that drops, suddenly you don't think much anymore.

When you don't think much anymore, then you'll see life as it is. When you see a person, you won't interpret that person, you won't see the image of the person. You won't have any racism or fear of a person. Everything you look at is as it is. There's no thinking about it. You're just seeing it as it is. Which means non-thought observation. Which means true observation.

Even a scientist understands that theoretically. They want to make sure that their observation is true, not contaminated by their previous judgements or knowledge about something. Because otherwise it will distort the result. The scientist wants to see something as it is, without their past projection or thoughts on it.

So you'll be seeing life as it is, with no thought.

Guess how you'll be seeing life? Like a newborn baby! But in an adult body. Your eyes won't be dull. Your eyes will sparkle like a newborn. You'll have so much interest in everybody, like a child who is a few years old—they're curious about everybody and everything.

When you see life as it is, life will be fascinating to you, and you'll understand why we came to this beautiful planet.

Otherwise, 'see life as it is', is just a few words. You cannot see things as they are if there are pre-judgements, or if you see things through rose-coloured glasses. That has to be cleared, and then you can see things as they are, and surrender to what is.

Why is it so hard to surrender sometimes?

Because we were trained in this society on our planet to hoard information. We are all hoarders.

Now, when a person hoards and collects all sorts of information, if someone tells them to get rid of it, they're not going to. It's going to be very, very difficult.

We're living in a society where we're just hoarding information and ideas, all the time. We want to come up with ideas, we want to get other people's ideas, and we want to hang onto our ideas.

And because of that training, it's very hard to let go of all the ideas that we've learned in life—about God, about others, about everything. We find it very hard to release that conditioning.

So we have to retrain how to surrender, how to let go of all those beliefs. When we realise they don't serve us, we just let them go.

Why is it difficult to surrender? Because we have been trained all our life to not surrender—to not let go of our ideas and conditioning. We have graduated with a PhD in Hoard-iculture! We are experts in hoarding concepts and beliefs.

We should take on a PhD of Empty-mology! That'll fix up all the hoarding, and surrender will be very easy once we master Emptymology.

Sacrifice

Can you explain sacrifice?

Nobody on this planet will sacrifice themself for anybody else unless they love them. You see, when we sacrifice ourself for others we are sacrificing our comfort, our abundance, our wealth, our precious time—we are sacrificing our life.

Can you see, in just those few examples I've shared, it feels like you're losing something. You're losing your wealth, you're losing your time. Who's going to do that?

We do it because we love others. So a mother or father of a newborn will sacrifice their life, their time, their wealth, for their baby. Nappy costs add up pretty quickly!

I've never had children, but many of my brothers and sisters do have children, and they all sacrifice when there is a newborn. They have to work during the day, and at night they have to wake up and feed the baby and change the nappies and fall back to sleep as quickly as possible. Suddenly they're not sleeping as much, so they're sacrificing their sleep too. Why do they do it if they're losing all this? Because they love their child.

And when they do this, what does it give them? Great joy. In that sacrifice, in that hardship, the father and mother might have sleepy eyes, but their hearts are not sleepy. Their hearts are celebrating about the newborn. They're so happy.

So in the same way, if we want to be deeply happy, we should love the world and sacrifice our life for everybody on the planet. Don't only sacrifice your life for a newborn—love everybody and sacrifice your life for everybody. Then you're going to be happy. You're going to be so happy that you don't even know how you became that happy!

But don't live your life that way just because I'm telling you. Live that way from your wise understanding and from experimenting with living that way. There has never been a time on the planet when somebody who sacrificed their life like that did not become tremendously happy.

Sacrifice—what a beautiful thing. Look at the whole of nature. Everything is sacrificing. The male Australian marsupial mouse will die within a week after it mates. They contribute so that the marsupial mice can continue, and then they drop dead. Even that is a sacrifice! Imagine all the guys out there knowing that they're going to drop dead after one contribution. Who's going to contribute? They won't! But the marsupial mouse does.

The whole of nature is sacrificing. The coconut tree is dropping its fruit. Its fruit gives water, the husk can be made into a bowl afterwards to eat food from. You can get coconut oil out of it. You can eat the flesh, and the stringy fibre can be made into ropes. It just constantly drops its fruit and sacrifices itself. Constantly, everything is sacrificing itself like that.

So when we sacrifice ourself it's not disharmonious with nature. We're actually living in harmony with nature.

Don't be afraid to sacrifice, because it will transform you into a beautiful human being.

The attitude of 'I know'

When I hear what you have to say, I always get the feeling that I don't know anything. But I still have a tendency to feel I do know so many things. Could you talk about the attitude of 'I know' and how that affects our life.

You see, we're living in a world where we're forced to have the appearance that we know. For example, on your first day at a new job you have to look like you're confident.

After I graduated from university I worked in an accounting firm, and after two and a half months they sent me out on my own to a client to do an audit. So what did I do? I had to bluff that I knew what I was doing—but I had no idea what I was doing!

So I sat down, wasting half an hour, thinking, "What am I trying to do here?" I was so new that I literally had to make up an approach! So I wrote down some questions that I needed to ask the client, and then I thought, "Should I ask all these questions? I'll bring them just in case I don't know what I'm doing when I get there." I had to bluff my way through it.

So I go to the client with the questions and I ask the questions and it all seems fine. The client doesn't know that I have no idea!

So we're living in a world where we're forced to put on an appearance that we know, otherwise we'll lose our job.

We don't say to the client, "I'm so sorry but I've only been at this company for two and a half months, this is the first time they've sent me out on my own. Please have compassion for me—I'll do my best, but can you try to understand if I make some mistakes?" If you do that you're going to lose your job!

See, this world doesn't accept that—even though that's the truth.

So we're trained to have the attitude that we know. Even if we don't know!

That 'I know' attitude might work in life—of course, after six months or a year in the job you start to know what you're doing and that's fine. But in this field of spirituality, that is so detrimental to the goal of happiness. Because if you are unhappy, you bluff to show other people that you're happy. So you're constantly pretending, and you never actually look at the root cause of your unhappiness in order to fix it.

So we go through life with this habit of, "I know. I'm confident. I know." We read two or three spiritual books—now we know everything about spirituality and we start to tell our friends about spirituality. We do a couple of meditation classes, and feel we know a lot about meditation.

See, we're trained that way.

Now the problem with that is we delude ourself, so we'll never actually change our perspective in life. We never look at the reality of ourself—"Why does my life feel monotonous and meaningless? Why? What's wrong with this world? Why do I feel no-one loves me? Something's wrong."

If we haven't got the courage to discuss this with a friend or someone, at least have the courage to contemplate this ourselves. And then from the, "I know everything," we will feel, "Wow, I don't know anything."

Before this, we feel, "I went through the education system—primary school, high school, university. I got good results, I'm educated, I'm smart. My family looks up to me as someone that knows what they're doing, someone who's sharp and smart."

But when we are honest with ourself, we will realise, "Wow, I don't know. What's wrong with me? Why aren't I happy? What's wrong with me?"

So when we begin to doubt our false confidence, this puts us into a feeling that—"It might be that I don't know how to be happy. It might be. Because with all my qualifications and this and that, I still don't feel happy."

And then suddenly, in that sincerity, there's power. That's absolute power. Then automatically you start to want to change whatever needs to be changed. When you speak to others, you won't bluff.

If the whole world was honest, one person would open up, "I don't know why, but I'm just not happy." And other people would say, "I feel the same!" You'd hear another person in the second aisle at the supermarket saying, "I feel the same!" Another one says, "I feel the same!" The person working at the checkout screams, "I feel the same!" The Manager in the deli section thinks, "I feel the same! How can we all feel like this?"

And then a little child at the checkout with their mum says, "Maybe we don't know what we're doing."

So that, "I know, I know," is very, very harmful for change.

Now, if the status quo on this planet is that people are feeling light and grateful for life, feeling love in their heart, and feeling that life's just beautiful, then why would we want to change? We wouldn't need to change.

But if we're feeling unhappy on a mass scale, because of the habit of thinking we know everything—bluffing ourselves like I bluffed when I worked in the accounting firm—then we need to change. If we want to be happy, we need to change.

It's not that we *need* to change, because *need* to change sounds like someone is forcing you. No. We should *love* to change.

I'll share something—I loved to change when I was a spiritual seeker. I had anger problems, and I loved to just stop that, because I wasn't happy. I wished to be happy, so I wanted to change.

And I knew, "I don't know." I might have bluffed at the accounting firm, but in my life I did not bluff. I felt, "I don't know. And I want to speak to someone that knows. I want to live with someone that knows. I want to see what true knowing looks like."

It seems logical that over time, the more you contemplate deeply and the more you become happy, you will come to know more, right? No. The truth is the more you progress, the more you feel you don't know.

So enlightenment is when you know that you know nothing. And because you know nothing, you're happy! Like a newborn child. The child knows nothing—that's why they're so happy. So, ironically, as you contemplate, as you practise, you start to know, "I know nothing."

Don't go the other way around—"The more I know, the more happy I am." Because we have all lived that way. All I'm saying is—be careful. We might end up being flat, totally depressed, with no energy, no spring, and feeling no purpose for living.

Our mantra in life should be, 'The less I know, the more happy I am'.

Conditioning

You've said that shedding our conditioning is a process that takes time. Could you give some guidance or encouragement to people who are going through that process?

If it takes a person ten hours to drive from Brisbane to Sydney, it's going to take roughly ten hours to drive back. It's not going to take five hours. So in the same way, it took us many, many years to build up all this conditioning.

Conditioning simply means ideas or concepts or rules that cause problems like emotional instability or difficult situations. These ideas will cause us to suffer when the right conditions occur.

So it takes many, many years to build up this conditioning. It takes a lot of movies—*Rambo, Rocky, Terminator, Commando,* Bruce Lee movies—to build up this feeling that fighting is cool, violence is fun. Watching just one of these movies is not going to build up the conditioning.

And it's not only movies that cause us to pick up conditionings of violence. You can imagine the rest. How many years do we watch the news and see those violent stories? Then you've got computer games where you pretend you are a character and you're punching and killing the other characters.

So it takes a lot. It didn't happen in one or two hours.

If a person wants an overnight miracle to wash away all their conditioning so they become as gentle as the Buddha and as loving as Jesus, it's not going to happen! It takes many, many years to get rid of the violence in us.

And that's just conditioning related to violence. It takes many years to build up all sorts of conditioning. For example, the conditionings that make us feel that we are a failure. It's not going to happen overnight or in one week or one year. Because we are all divine, we are all 'God', you see, so to convince God that God is a failure—it takes a lot! It's like trying to convince an elephant that it's very small. It's not easy—it's going to take many years.

So we have to be very patient, we have to be methodical, we have to be logical, we have to be realistic. Then, with that attitude, we will approach it intelligently—learning the fastest way to purify or burn away these conditionings so that all the Rocky punches, all the bazooka machine gun shooting, all the Terminators, all the Commandos, get removed.

So to let go of that conditioning we come up with a fast, intelligent approach, and then we practise that.

It does take time. Even the fastest way takes time. It takes a lot of practice and it's not something that happens very quickly. Even when we're doing it in the fastest way possible, it still takes time.

Now, is it good to have the understanding that I just shared? Yes, it's very good, because with that understanding we won't have unrealistic expectations which lead to disappointment and giving up. If our expectation is not realistic, we can lose faith when we don't see the expected results.

So in conclusion, make sure that your method for getting rid of conditioning has been tested and that it really works. Make sure there are Masters that have tried those methods and they worked. Then you adopt those methods and practise them—give it your best effort, and be patient.

How does being in the presence of an enlightened Master remove or purify karma and conditioning in a disciple?

In the presence of love, negativity will just be destroyed.

All the suffering in the world—conditioning, karma, etc—is caused by not feeling, perceiving or knowing the innate love in our heart. And a Master knows that innate love, so just being in their presence will destroy our conditioning, our negativities.

You don't really know how the process works, but you feel lighter. You feel more natural. You don't feel you are the weird one. You feel beautiful as you are. You won't feel the need to enhance yourself. A good hairdo won't enhance you. A new set of clothes won't enhance you. You just feel beautiful as you are. Just by being in the presence of that love.

You see, our conditioning, negativities, or karma all come from this doubt of who we are. How do you know when you have doubt about who you are? You know because there's a sense of confusion, like, "I don't know what to do with my life." Or— "I'm not sure which job I should take, I'm not sure if I should get married or not, I'm not sure which school I should go to, I'm not sure who I should ask to the school formal. I'm not sure who I am." Just confusion!

Well, the Master's knowing of who they are is a direct knowing. It's not evidence-based. It's not based on how many students they have or how many best-selling books they have written or how rich or poor they are. It's got nothing to do with those things. It's just a direct knowing of who they truly are.

That knowing is so powerful that in their presence a person's confusion will be bowled over by it. Like if an elephant is running along a path and you jump in the way, you'll be bowled over. Their knowing is so powerful that if a million confused people jump in front of them, all their confusion will be bowled over—by one Master.

So in that presence, you won't have confusion. What does that mean? That means you get a sense of clarity. You feel there's nothing to work out. It's like the Master's sense of knowing rubs onto you.

When you have more of that clarity, then your conditioning must be clearing, because it's the conditioning that causes the confusion.

So essentially, the Master's presence and the power of the Master's direct knowing will clear your conditioning and karma.

Seeking recognition

Why do we so often seek recognition or success or fame?

Because we don't know who we are. If you don't know who you are then it's only natural to try to prove yourself.

Let's take for example Rafael Nadal, in tennis. If Rafael Nadal visits his local tennis club to have a hit with his friend, would he say to people at the club, "Do you want to come and check out my backhand?" When he plays on the court, will he hit the backhand in a way to show off to people watching? I know I did that when I played tennis as a kid! But he wouldn't, because he knows he's a champion tennis player. He knows he's one of the world's best, so he doesn't feel the need to prove that he's a great tennis player.

When I was young I played social tennis every Sunday in Rockdale, and when some players hit the ball it was more like dancing than hitting a tennis ball. The moves were all extra dramatic. We were just innocent, enjoying tennis, but there was an intention to show off—"Look at me. I'm a great tennis player." That's because we knew we weren't the best tennis players in the world.

That is tennis. But in this field, every single one of us is the best in the world. Equal best. As God's creations, we are all the absolute best. But we don't believe it.

We don't become the best by convincing millions that we are the best. Rafael Nadal is not trying to convince anybody, because he already knows he is the best. In the same way, the power of just knowing who we really are will remove all our doubts and negativities.

So when we don't know who we are, then the proving begins, in the form of attention seeking. And the nature of some of the attention seeking can take a whole lifetime to prove. Proving that you're successful in business can take a whole lifetime. Proving that you're talented in music could take a whole lifetime.

So that's why we seek recognition, success and fame—because we know not who we are.

Suffering

Is it necessary to have pain and suffering in our own life so that we can get to a point where we will seek to end our suffering?

It's not necessary in theory, but in practice it seems to be.

You see, we tend to learn by touching the hot stove—"Ooh, I shouldn't touch the hot stove with my hand!" We tend to learn by suffering.

And when we don't have suffering, we learn things, but we learn at a very surface level.

When we have suffering in our life, we become deeper. We seem to have more understanding of others and we are more able to feel the feelings of another.

If you've never gone for a job interview and never received any rejection letters, then when your friend goes for a job interview and gets a rejection letter, you could never know how that feels—the feeling of failure. You can't understand. You can't relate to your friend.

So in that sense, suffering may not be necessary but it seems to do the job. All the great, beautiful beings on the planet, who are the light of the world, have had lives of massive suffering—so much suffering that they fell in love with humanity.

They can relate to humanity. They can feel how other people feel. They can feel the heavy burden of this planet—and suddenly in their heart they just want to do the best they can for the rest of their life to make a difference to people's lives.

Nobody will have that feeling if there's no suffering.

I'm not saying you should 'seek' suffering, but suffering is often quite a beautiful thing. Suffering can be your greatest teacher and your greatest friend.

You see, if you have a lot of suffering in your life, then when other types of suffering come, it's no big deal. But if your life is totally protected by your parents or by society, then when you go through your first relationship break-up it's going to feel like hell. Whereas if you've had a lot of suffering in your life, it's not going to be a joy to go through a break-up, but you're going to have a lot more spiritual strength to cope with it.

So from that perspective, our life should not be focussed on trying to minimise suffering—trying to find the situations of least suffering in our life. That is not how to make the most of our life in this world.

What we want to do is be open and embrace life, embrace the good and the bad. When suffering comes, welcome that, and have the strength to make the most out of it so it turns you into a more beautiful human being.

It was only through suffering in my life that I came to love humanity. My mother died when I was three years old, I spent a year as a child in a refugee camp in Malaysia, I lived a life of financial poverty—always just enough to eat, to survive, but financially poor. And it made me love people. When somebody gives me one little thing, I feel, "Wow, what beautiful kindness."

So don't be afraid of suffering. No great person became beautiful and great without suffering.

Why does suffering seem to change people in such a positive way sometimes?

Because suffering can make you real. And happiness, positivity, joyfulness, etc, can only come to a person who's real and true to themself—what you see is what you get. In other words, not a pretender, not a bluffer, not a trickster.

It's like going to a shop and there's a sign in the window saying, 'Everything is 50% off'. You see some shirts reduced from $30 down to $15—that's a bargain! So you go in and they say, "All the shirts are sold out except for two, which are size XXXL. The rest is new stock at full price." So what you see is not what you get. When you go inside, it's different, it's not real. You've been tricked, you've been bluffed.

So it is the suffering in life that makes us more real, and helps us to develop courage to just be ourselves—it doesn't matter if the whole world doesn't like the way we are. We might be financially poor, we may not be educated, we might have a resume that shows nothing but failures, but we don't hide that, we don't cover it up. We're just comfortable as we are.

Suffering will make you tired of pretending—you're done with it. You haven't got energy for acting and you don't feel comfortable acting.

So life will destroy all your pretension, your acting, your bluffing, and it leaves a grounded person, a fearless person.

Understanding that, we should embrace suffering. It's probably a big 'should'! It's easy to say 'embrace suffering', but when cancer suddenly strikes it's very difficult to embrace it. But always know there must be some good in this. Always have that attitude—"Everything in life happens for the best, so my suffering must be for the best."

I'll share something with you—in this world, no human being became a great, beautiful human being when their life was just easy, with no suffering.

I know a life of hardship did me such good. From a young age, in my first year of high school, I had to catch the bus home quickly to cook for my father and my older brother. Seven days a week I cooked for them and did the dishes, and a lot of times I'd do the shopping too.

I made the same lunch to take to school every day. I would bring two oranges and I'd fry some eggs to have with bread. If I didn't have time to make the eggs, I'd just bring three oranges.

And where did I get the oranges? I would ride my BMX bike to Banana Joe's fruit shop in Marrickville and buy a box of oranges. I would put the box on the frame of the bike and while I was pedalling I had to balance the box with my legs so it didn't fall off. When I got home without the box falling off, I tell you, it was an absolute relief!

My father had a car, but he wouldn't drive. He'd make me go and get it—"If you want your lunch, you go and get the oranges."

It might sound cruel, but it was so good for me, because now I'm not afraid of hardship.

The hardship prepared me for life. And when it came to spiritual practice, I could practise with endurance. I was not afraid to give it everything I had. And when I saw something that showed the way to be happy, I'd be excited about it. I'd take it with both hands.

So we should embrace suffering, we should not be afraid of it. To go through this life trying to avoid suffering—that is not the way to live. Because nobody can escape the events and circumstances that can cause suffering in this world.

It's up to us to decide if we let the suffering turn us into something beautiful or into something bitter. But suffering certainly has the potential to make us real, make us down-to-earth, make us grounded, make us transparent, make us gentle, make us humble, make us strong—make us happy.

If someone wishes to be out of poverty, but that doesn't happen, does that mean at some level their soul really wants to be in poverty?

You see, when we say we wish to be out of poverty, there are many, many layers. In the deepest part of us, it's perfection.

The soul doesn't see poverty as a bad thing. Remember the soul is not a material thing. And to the soul, a material thing has no real good or bad. So the soul doesn't see richness as being better than poverty. That's the first thing we have to be very clear about.

Secondly, the soul has an agenda. Often we don't know what that agenda is. A lot of greatness, strength, beauty and magic in a human being comes through the blessings of a poverty background. If the soul didn't go through that poverty background, it wouldn't shape the person in that way.

So at a deep level, the soul—or our true Self—knows what it's doing, knows its agenda. And that agenda has nothing to do with good or bad.

So we should be careful and never be quick to judge that poverty is bad or good.

At the end of the day, the deepest wish will be fulfilled. And if someone lives a whole life of poverty, it must be that soul's wish to experience the greatness in that.

So we shouldn't look down at or judge someone in poverty. But that doesn't mean that we can't see an opportunity in that person's poverty. Sometimes that soul comes to experience poverty so they can give another person a gift—an opportunity for the other person to express their love by helping them.

Finding happiness

If happiness is something that comes from within us, why do we feel so happy when, for example, we're spending time with friends or we're watching a baby walk for the first time—things that are actually outside of us?

See, that is happiness too. Our friends make us happy. To see our baby walk for the first time makes us happy.

But the problem with that is it's only partial happiness, or temporary happiness. Because if the person you called a friend suddenly cheats on you, disturbance will come. And when your baby walks—"Oh, that's beautiful!" But if the baby falls and breaks their leg, you will feel disturbance.

So is it happiness? Yes, it's happiness, but partial. It's temporary.

So it's better to have full happiness, where, for example, we hang around with our dear friend, which gives us great joy, and if the friend cheats on us, our happiness is still not affected.

That's full happiness. That's not partial. It's hard for our mind to comprehend that because it seems impossible. But it is possible.

Why are some people naturally positive while others are negative or moody?

There are many factors, but to be positive, to be happy, is actually a skill.

When you learn the skill to be positive, the result is that your life will be very beautiful, very happy. It doesn't matter what a person knows—if their life is not happy, they don't know that skill. It's simple. It doesn't matter how smart they are, how strong they are, what they have or what they don't have—it's a skill.

And every skill on this planet requires training. I don't know anyone that is really good at anything without being trained. If you want to be a skilful chef, you have to train. You have to pull out the recipe book and start cooking. You have to learn how much salt or chilli is too much, and you need to practise. If you learn from a master chef, you don't make as many mistakes— they teach you about the mistakes they've already made. Then you can learn the skill more quickly.

So you need training.

If someone is negative and not happy, they see the world as bleak, and they see how unfortunate their life is. They might feel, "Why was I born in a family like that?" "Why do I have my father's genes—he's so short! I'm going to be short like him." I used to think with this type of negativity! Why not think, "A lot of saints are very short." You're not going to be a champion basketball player if you're short, but you have potential to become a saint!

Do we blame somebody who's a poor chef? No. They just don't have the skill, that's all. A person may be a poor chef, but one day they could be a great chef.

I always say Roger Federer was not a champion tennis player the first day he came on the tennis court. He wouldn't have known how to hit the ball properly or how to do aces. So he learnt that skill—through training, dedication, sacrifice, endurance, determination, dreams, hopes and practice.

So the person who is negative just doesn't have that skill of being happy, or if they know it a little, they haven't been trained to be very good at it—very good at being calm, very good at being relaxed amidst chaos in life, very good at being detached when life events and circumstances smash them. It's just a skill.

We either know that skill or we don't. And when we know that skill, the next question is—how practiced are we at it? How rehearsed are we at it? That's all.

How can we best give up bodily attachment, or addiction to outer pleasure?

By knowing what leads to happiness and what doesn't.

Let's say a person's goal is to be a millionaire, and they have some money to make property investments. Now, one property might give a maximum yield—including rental income and capital gains—of 15% per annum, and another property might have a maximum yield of 5%.

So if the person's goal is to be a millionaire quickly, would it be hard for the person to decide which property to invest in? No. The main effort is to work out which property has the better yield. It takes time and effort to research, but once the research is done it's an easy decision—you're going to invest in the one that has a higher yield. It's very simple.

So, the question is asking how people can stop seeking pleasurable things and desires. It's very easy if they know that the yield, in terms of happiness, is very little. Then they'll just stop. No-one will need to inspire them to stop chasing things that give outer pleasure—the decision will be very easy.

But who can convince them? If a person believes that they're going to get a very high yield of happiness by seeking outer pleasure—outer achievements, fame and fortune, recognition and appreciation, wealth and abundance—who can convince them not to do that? Nobody! No God or saint can do it.

The only way the person can realise the true yield is to go through a whole lifetime—or many lifetimes—and check the balance in their bank account of happiness. When they see it's in negative, then they realise that wasn't a good investment. And then the next lifetime, or maybe the next year, they look for different ways to invest their time to get a high yield of happiness.

On this planet we have witnessed a lot of people who have chased big desires like fame and fortune. We see evidence in books and magazines, on TV and through word of mouth. And those who have fulfilled those desires look like they are admired—"Wow, that is the ideal."

The evidence that we're seeing tells us it's a very high yield, so we pursue that way of living, just assuming that's the way to happiness.

If that's what we witness, it's very hard to convince someone to just surrender, to not chase any fame or fortune, and to have the attitude that, 'If fame or fortune comes, just let it come, but don't chase it, don't salivate for it. If it comes, let it come, and if it goes, let it go.'

Who is going to believe that the highest yield will come from investing all their time and vitality in learning the art to let go, to surrender, to be flexible like water, to know that everything that comes is the will of God? It's very hard to believe that. Why? Because we don't have much evidence of that—there are not many people we can witness to see the high yield in that.

But if we are very fortunate, if we're an astute investor, we check our bank account all the time. We check the annual performance and we see that, "Overall, I wasn't happy this year." And the next year—"Oh, again I wasn't really happy. I'm not getting a good return—I'd better change the way I'm investing."

Some people are very lucky like that. They're very astute. Then they make the change to invest in a high yield alternative. They try to look for those people who have a high yield, and they ask them, "Where do you place your time? Where do you invest all your daily energy?" And then they'll follow that. They'll put their investment there.

They'll start to meditate and they'll ignore all the people who say, "Don't waste your time meditating, you're too busy, you haven't got time to meditate." They won't believe that, because they've already made their investment the other way and it didn't bring a great yield.

So the most important thing is to make sure you invest your time and energy somewhere that has a high yield of happiness.

Doesn't searching for happiness just perpetuate an unhappy feeling because it comes from the thought that, "I'm not a happy person"? Happiness seems to be a goal very much in the Western world, where people have abundance yet they still consider themself lacking. Simple people in poorer countries are very happy and content. People with less seem to be more happy in general, and people with more are searching for so-called happiness, but it seems like an elusive goal.

Amma said beautifully—"The difference between the rich and the poor is that the poor people are crying and suffering in their dirt huts, and the rich people are crying and suffering in their air-conditioned mansions."

It's true that in the poorer countries—like Asian countries, India, Vietnam—you tend to see people slightly happier than the more wealthy people in the West. This is because their life is just more simple and because they have more family closeness, so loneliness is much less of an issue. If you eliminate loneliness and you eliminate the deadline-related stress in life, you will see people are a lot more happy.

But in those poorer countries, they actually don't think of their life as happier. If they get a chance to go to the West they'll jump at it straight away. So they're not aware of being happier.

In the West, many people are reading books on how to be happy, like personal development books and books that talk about living a balanced lifestyle. On the other hand, most people in the more simple countries have never read books on happiness, and they haven't learned anything about happiness, but they're a lot more happy.

So it looks like people in the West are chasing happiness, trying to be happy, and yet Australia, for example, has one of the highest teenage suicide rates in the world. Why? Is that because the search for happiness leads to unhappiness? No. It's because there's an error in the research about happiness, which has led to an error in the result.

Let me give you an example. Let's say there are two people in a race. One person is sitting still in one spot, and another person is driving a Lamborghini. Now let's say the winner of the race is whoever goes the furthest north, and the person who has a Lamborghini drives at high speed, but gets lost and starts heading south. So the person who is sitting still, not moving anywhere, will win the race because they are further north.

In this situation, can you say that the person sitting still is a better driver? No, because they haven't even jumped in the car. But they won the race because the other person went the wrong way.

So in these poor countries, it's like they're sitting still, not searching for happiness, and they're more happy just because they're not going backwards, searching the wrong way—whereas in the West we're searching, but we're going backwards.

You see, perfect happiness is a state of perfect contentment, but if you are trying to fulfil desires then that means you have certain conditions that have to be met before you can be content.

How can you be content if you need to meet conditions? Some conditions are actually impossible to achieve.

It's not rocket science to work out that to be happy all we have to do is stop believing that we have to meet conditions in order to be happy. So driving in the right direction means training to control the mind—to control the thoughts that make us a slave to our desires.

And that is the whole spiritual life. If a person is not skilled at wrestling against this pull to meet all these conditions, then they'll be bowled over. They'll be pulled like a slave, trying to meet conditions for their whole life.

So it's not accurate to say that the searching for happiness leads to unhappiness. It's more accurate to say there's an error in the way we are searching. Because once you learn what actually leads to happiness, then your whole energy will be practicing to be content. Every time you feel a pull to be famous or to achieve, you tell yourself, "No, I won't chase that, I'll just relax. I'll just let that go."

That's why someone can attain enlightenment even if they are sitting in a cave for six or seven years. Externally, they haven't achieved anything, but internally they attained contentment.

In the cave, sometimes they thought, "What am I doing in this cave? I'm being bitten by insects, I'm cold and uncomfortable. What am I doing here? I should go and look for somewhere comfortable—I'm wasting my life away."

But they'll know, "Aha, I'll let that go. I'll let those thoughts go." They keep on letting them go, letting them go, until they

155

conquer every thought. Then they walk out shining, content, light and glowing in perfect happiness.

So be alert, and check that you're going the right way—do you feel content? Do you feel light? At the end of every day, before you go to bed, you should check. A business person will check the profits at the end of each day. In the same way, you should check every day—do you feel content and light? If not, why? What conditions are you trying to fulfil?

Now, I did not say fame or fortune are bad. Those things are neutral, not bad. Look at the Dalai Lama—he's very famous, but he's very, very happy. And there are many people who are as happy as the Dalai Lama, and hardly anyone knows them. So you can see, it's not about fame or not fame. It's about contentment.

Sometimes when you live a simple life you just don't know what you are missing out on, so you don't have thoughts about what you lack!

When I grew up, I didn't know there were families that went on holidays. It just didn't enter my mind that you might go on holidays with your family. As a matter of fact, in my family after we came to Australia we used to say, "Why are these Westerners always going on holidays, wasting their money?" We used to think like this!

So when you don't know what you're missing out on, you're more content. The people who live in the dirt huts just don't know they haven't got an iPad. They don't know they haven't got the latest model mobile phone—they're OK with a cheap old phone. So therefore they're content—they're happy.

Learning from a Master

How can I love myself when I feel like I have so many weaknesses and shortcomings?

Hang around with people that love themself. Be good friends with them, open your heart to them. Wash the dishes for them, mow their lawn, bake them a cake, hang their clothes out. Do that for ten years and let's see if you find it difficult to love yourself after that. It will be impossible!

The ancient Masters knew that is the best way. That's why they created 'satsang'. Satsang basically means 'in reverence, at the feet of the Master'. What does 'at the feet of the Master' mean? Well, to be at someone's feet means you're pretty close. And in that closeness, over many occasions, something happens. You start to become like the Master, and over time you transform into a Master yourself.

What comes to me now is that game of tug-of-war. Two groups are pulling each end of a rope and there's a line in the middle. Whichever one is stronger will pull the weaker side across that line.

So it's like a tug-of-war between the person at the feet of the Master, and the Master. The person is pulling towards negativity, trying to convince the Master, and the Master is pulling towards positivity or happiness. If you lose, you will become the Master.

So in this game of tug-of-war, when you win you lose, and when you lose you win! If you out-pull the Master and you win, you lose. Because you will become egotistic and unhappy. You won't have the wisdom, the love, the strength, the courage, the gratitude and the joy. If you win, you won't have those things—if you lose, you'll have them.

So in my case, when I spent time with my Master, I immediately said, "Master, I'll lose straight away!" I didn't even bother pulling the tug-of-war, I just dived on the other side straight away!

So if you hang around the Master like that, you'll love yourself automatically. There has never been a time in history that this didn't work.

If someone has chosen to take on the guidance of a Spiritual Master and that Spiritual Master does something that the student feels is wrong, how can we let go in that moment where there's that tug-of-war happening?

Let's assume that they are a true Master—in India they call them a 'Satguru' or a 'Buddha'. That means somebody who has mastered their mind. In other words, someone who has perfect equanimity or perfect happiness.

Now when we spend time with someone like that, we will have this tug-of-war, we will have this resistance. The mind will always resist—that's its duty. The mind's job description is 'Must cause misery'. It says, "Don't believe anybody, don't trust anybody!"

So that's the job description of the mind. Its role is to cause misery.

Now, it is good to know that, because then we are prepared. So when we do feel miserable, we're not surprised. You won't be surprised because you know the mind is just doing its thing. If you feel depressed or you feel lonely, you're not surprised. Something in you will know, "Oh, I see, the mind is doing its work."

Then we are prepared for it—"OK, if the mind is doing that all the time, which I don't enjoy, I have to be prepared, I have to know how to counteract that, I have to be able to beat the mind in this battle, I have to be stronger in this wrestling match."

When I was four or five years old in Vietnam, sometimes I'd get into a wrestling match with other kids. We didn't have punch ups and stuff like that but we had wrestling matches. I was kind of stronger than everyone else my age, so I would give them a headlock and I'd say, "Do you give in?" Then I'd hold them until they said, "I give in!" So I'd let them go, and that person wouldn't try to wrestle with me next time.

We have to be prepared to wrestle with the mind like that. We have to give the mind a headlock—"Do you give in? You're not going to cause me trouble anymore are you?" Until it screams, "I won't cause any more trouble, I promise!" Then you let it go.

So having this understanding of the nature of the mind makes us prepared. It literally prepares us for life.

When we resist learning from the Master, that's the same—the mind is doing its thing. Because if you're learning from the Master and hanging around the Master, the mind will do everything it can to make you stop that. It will throw everything at you, because its role or job description is to make you miserable. And if you hang around the Master you will not be miserable. So the mind will resist. It will come up with all sorts of nonsense.

If we are prepared for that and have that understanding, then we have a better chance to override the mind. Instead of co-operating with it, we do what's clear, we do what makes sense.

See, the mind always makes you very vague and confused, and the Master always makes it very clear. This is the process of training.

Of course, the Master will prescribe techniques to shut down the mind, to slam the door in its face, but the mind will try to convince you, "Don't listen to the Master—resist!"

So it comes down to clear understanding, faith and endurance. Then you will be able to master your mind.

What's the most precious thing that you learned from your Guru?

I learned so much.

For example, even if I'd heard or read something before, if my Guru said the same thing, that was of critical importance, because after I heard my Guru say it, I'd start to have 100% conviction.

Before that, no matter how many books I'd read, even if I trusted something and believed it, there was not 100% conviction. But after Amma spoke about it, I'd have total conviction.

So what does 100% conviction do to you? It makes you not fluff around. We all fluff around, including myself when I was a seeker! I'd go check out different things, try to figure out what's the best way, trying this and that. That wastes so much time. You could spend years doing that.

But once the Master says, "This is how it is..." then I will practise straight away. I will live it straight away. And when I live it, I start to cry in great joy—because my Master's words prove so true. Things are exactly like she says. So you start to feel such gratitude and you live it more and more. You don't waste time.

Self-realisation, enlightenment, moksha, salvation—these are just words for the goal of spirituality. But just being with the Master, seeing the Master with my own eyes, made me feel love for that goal. Even though I was only one amongst thousands with the Master, it still made me feel love for the goal and know that the goal was real—it's not some funny thing somebody made up.

Well, when you know that in your heart, it does something to you. When you're clear about that, you start to walk more purposefully, more clearly. There's less guesswork. Just being around Amma gave me this innocent feeling that, "I can be like that."

You're not telling this to other people. You're not being egotistic and thinking, "I'm going to achieve self-realisation," or, "I'm going to be enlightened." It's not in a weird way like that. Just quietly in your heart you feel, "I can live like that. I can be like that."

One has to have that feeling before enlightenment can happen. If that is not there, enlightenment won't come. There's a feeling that comes that, "It's possible for me." Not that, "I will achieve this,"—if you think, "I will achieve this," know that's your mind. I'm talking about the feeling that, "I might be able to achieve this." That feeling. And it seems real.

Well, Amma did that to me.

Of course that shaped my spiritual practice, that shaped my purposeful living to dedicate my life for the well-being of others. Basically, I was following my Master's teachings—chanting my mantra, always trying to put others first. I sacrificed my life. When somebody asked me to help them with something and my mind didn't want to, I'd tell my mind to shut up and I'd gladly help. I always made sure I had the last say, not my mind. And the last say would always be actions that benefit others.

So I was just living the Master's teachings. But all of that comes from being with Amma and the feeling inside me that, "I think I can live like that." If I was not living with Amma, seeing how she was living, seeing what it looks like, I don't think I would've had that absolute faith. I've always had a strong faith, but I don't think it would have been that absolute faith.

Knowing God

How can I love God when God doesn't give me what I want?

God always gives us what we want. Never in the history of this whole universe has God not given people what they want.

Let's say a person wants to have the strength and the endurance and the adventurous nature to climb Mount Everest. So they're saying to God, "God, give me the strength, show me the way to climb Mount Everest. That's what I want."

And then the person goes to the Himalaya region and there's a little earthquake there and they feel, "Wow, that's really dangerous." So they book a flight back home and never fly back to the Himalayas again, even after a decade without any earthquakes.

So the question is—did God give that person what they wanted? Absolutely. Because they didn't really want to climb Mount Everest. Their true goal was not to climb Mount Everest, or they would have done it.

So was that wish fulfilled? Absolutely. One cannot say God didn't fulfil that wish.

God doesn't only listen to the words we speak. God listens to our heart. What we speak in our heart, God knows. Whatever we wish for in our heart will come true. If we wish for it sincerely enough, it will come true. And if we change our mind, then that means we didn't truly wish for that, we wished for something else. For example, sometimes we think we love something, but when we try it we realise that our heart's not really in it. That shows it was never truly in our heart in the first place.

Never was there a wish in my heart that was not fulfilled. I had many wishes that were not fulfilled, but I can say, they were not my heart's wish. When I look back, I can see they were never truly my heart's wish.

What's the role and advantage of connecting with God in form as opposed to God in the formless?

It's whatever works.

Let's say a mother has to send her child to a hospital far away, and she has to drive five hours to visit the child. If the mother is driving home and she sees a billboard of an elephant in the zoo, the mother will immediately think of the child because the child loves elephants. So when the mother sees the elephant on the billboard she sees the child in the elephant, doesn't she? She doesn't see the elephant, she only sees her child. She'll smile as she remembers her child.

In the same way, whatever you see God as, God is.

So if you see God as that force that is formless—that invisible God—then you feel close to that invisible God, and that God will communicate to you in many different ways. God will use the formless aspect of God to manifest himself or herself.

And if a person sees God in form, that works as well. Some people are just not good at seeing the invisible. They find it easier to see something in the physical form. So therefore they might see God in the form of a human being, like their Master, and they feel closeness to God in that way.

Whichever method, it doesn't matter. What matters is it works—there is a feeling of closeness and refuge in this supreme power, there is a sense of feeling relaxed and peaceful knowing that, "My life's being taken care of in every little way."

Then, how can you not have peacefulness? It would be impossible, if you feel that type of safety in this supreme power that takes care of you and guides you. Then you're not going to worry about disease, you're not going to worry about not having enough money, you're not going to worry about not having friends, you're not going to worry that your life will have no purpose. You won't have anything like this, because you know, "God will give me what's best for me—God will take care of it."

In the same way, a child who goes to school doesn't worry about what's going to be in their lunchbox, because the child knows the mother is going to give the child the best. The child just gets their bag and says, "OK, let's go to school." Often the child only knows what's for lunch when they open up the lunchbox! They don't worry about it do they?

So when you have faith in God you will know that God will give you the best in this lunchbox of life. You'll just know that. So you will not worry, in the same way the child will not worry what's for lunch today.

It doesn't matter whether you worship God through form or formless—whatever is easier for you.

Spiritual community

*How important is it for a spiritual seeker to find themselves
a sangha or spiritual community?*

Anything that can help us is good.

It's like if we haven't got much money and we have to pay
a bill, we open up the piggy bank and it's just heavy with small
coins. Then you look in another bedroom and you find another
piggy bank, you get another fifty or sixty dollars of coins—
everything helps.

So being in a sangha or community helps. Helps tremendously.

The first help it gives is that you don't feel weird. If you're
doing spiritual practice in this world, people look at you like
you're weird. Friends look at you—"Weird." Family looks
at you—"Weird." The bus driver looks at you when you're
meditating in your seat at the back of the bus—"That's weird."

That will destroy your motivation to do spiritual practice. It
puts doubt in you—"How come no-one else is doing it? How
come I'm the only one?"

That's how I felt myself when I was on the spiritual path.
And I tell you what, I made sure I didn't bring it up at work or at
the tennis court! Because even though I was strong-minded and
I loved my path and I loved the goal of peacefulness, it doesn't
help when you have a lot of opposition that thinks you're weird.
So the sangha is fantastic.

When I went to Amma's sangha in India, suddenly I wasn't
weird anymore. Suddenly kindness, selflessness and present
moment practice were promoted and admired! That helps. That's
encouraging.

And when you forget to do spiritual practice there's always a person walking around with their mala doing spiritual practice. So you remember—you get your wrist mala, and do some mantra practice yourself.

So in a sangha, other people who have similar goals, who are similar minded, act as a trigger for you to remember. They help you. And every time you practise, you help them. You're almost challenging each other to defeat the mind. There's no opposition in this sport. It's actually your own mind that is the opposition.

In that sense, we all come together in a sangha so that we can help each other conquer our own minds. By ourself, sometimes it's challenging to conquer our mind, but group effort makes it a lot easier.

So the purpose of the sangha is to help us maximise the chance to have victory over our mind. And victory over our mind means we all become happy!

It is also tremendously beneficial for a sangha to have an enlightened Master to guide it. Because even if you have a sangha of a thousand people, it's possible that the whole thousand people get defeated by the mind. But with an enlightened Master, the Master makes sure the whole ship is going in the right direction towards peace, not destruction. The Master will make sure that victory will happen over our own mind.

About Sri Avinash

Sri Avinash was born in Nha Trang, a fishing village in South Vietnam, in 1973. His childhood was carefree in many ways, but there were also difficult times. His mother died in a vehicle accident when he was 3 years old, and he rarely saw his father who was a fisherman and spent most of his time at sea.

When Sri Avinash was 8 years old, his father escaped from the Vietnamese communist regime with his two sons. After a year in a refugee camp in Malaysia, they were eventually resettled in Australia.

His life in Sydney was challenged by a new language and culture, the absence of nurture from a mother, and poverty. But in his heart he always felt that each hardship he faced was good for him, sensing that it was somehow preparing him for a significant role in the future.

He went on to complete three university qualifications and tried various careers in Sydney. But it was when he realised his prestigious job in one of the 'Big Four' accounting firms was never going to fulfill his yearning for purpose and meaning that he chose to follow his heart and pursue a spiritual life instead. By now he was in his early 20's.

Sri Avinash was exposed to several Spiritual Masters on this journey, but in 2006 he became a disciple of Sri Mata Amritanandamayi (Amma, 'The Hugging Saint'). Under her guidance and inspiration, he chose to unreservedly commit his life to selfless service, meditation and sacrifice for the benefit of others.

While serving on Amma's 2009 Europe Tour, in Barcelona, Spain, his unrelenting focus on his practice resulted in him attaining the rare goal of self-realisation—also known as Buddhahood, enlightenment or Christ-consciousness.

Sri Avinash is a Bodhisattva—a Buddha of Compassion—an enlightened soul who chooses to return to the world again and again until all living beings are free from suffering. Out of his great compassion he travels the world blessing people with his darshan—transmitting divine love and spiritual power that removes people's suffering and awakens love in their lives.

The motto that drives Sri Avinash's Mission is 'Live to Love, Love to Serve'.

For information about Sri Avinash's teachings, books, retreats, courses, free events, distance and live healing sessions, Satori Transmission workshops and a schedule of his world tours, visit **www.SriAvinash.org**.